# Love Incarnate

Twenty Years After Awakening

Jan Frazier

For my beloved son and daughter

And for you, dear reader

May you come to know the
vastness of love

If the day and the night are such that you greet them with joy,
and life emits a fragrance like flowers and sweet-scented herbs,
is more elastic, more starry, more immortal,
– that is your success.

Henry David Thoreau

# Table of Contents

# Prelude

All my life I have been a writer. No writing project has daunted me like this one, the attempt to find words for my recent inner reality. It's why I've held back: the certainty that words are doomed to fail. Even to contemplate entering the terrain, I go into a stall; for to approach the task of articulating is necessarily to engage the mind, where words and ideas exist. It's to assemble sentences, one leading to another. Language asks us to enter into the realm of time, which words and sequential thought depend upon.

In the condition I would portray, these familiar human modes (time, idea, language) are not operative. Whether in writing or in spoken word, any attempt to render my interior swiftly dissolves into silence. Musical expression might come nearer, but I am – alas – no Fauré, no Brahms.

The articulation of this state of consciousness would daunt any writer, no matter the skill level. When contemplating whether to take on the challenge, I had to reckon with this: how much I would have to leave the preferred mode of being, sufficient to organize thoughts and chapters, to assemble sentences.

Other things have made me hesitant. The halting portrayal, were it to come about, inevitably would be misunderstood, misapplied. Likely it would generate more questions, in the minds of spiritual seekers, than answers.

As if any of this were about something as definitive as answers.

Why now am I trying anyhow? Something moves me to bear witness: simply that. To say (however imperfectly) *This is how it is,* for one embodied human being.

What is that *it?* It's how life can be once time (and the self it spawns) has ceased to feel substantial.

I recently stood at the rim of the Grand Canyon. How to fathom its vastness? How does a mere human being not dissolve to powder in its presence? However hard the earnest eyes and skin (the heart!) may strain to take it in.

Let alone articulate it.

Being there is to be in the presence of what is beyond time, or perhaps what contains all of time. If you have stood there, if you have drunk in the magnificence of that view, you may have some sense of the challenge facing me now.

Against all good reason not to, I am moved to try, to pay halting homage to a "place" of comparable vastness and beauty.

# First Things First

# Two Births

Once in a great while, we are given two births in a single life. There's the one the body has, at its start, with its eventual giving rise to the sense of self, and all that entails. The hands regularly run themselves over that self, getting the lay of the land as it learns what it is to be a somebody. The body, with its animal nature, carries on with its innate drive to keep alive. This enables the species to make more of itself, which must be a good thing.

The parallel upkeep of the burgeoning collection of values and beliefs, longings and so on, comes to carry as strong a wish for continuance as the body has had from the start: the persistence of breath in and breath out, hunger demanding to be relieved, thirst to be slaked. Only thing is, while water and food and oxygen are elemental needs (along with the hunger to be tenderly held), the self that's become convinced it can be subject to mortal danger is simply buying into the story it's been repeating from the early days (and nobody "out there" ever seems to indicate it could be otherwise, regarding the matter of who "you" are). The self insists, *I am real. I matter. I cannot stand to be threatened. To have the foundation pulled from beneath me is to cease to be.*

All of that is what inevitably comes with the first birth (the one common to us all) since we're influenced by those around us, and steadily shaped by life experience.

If a person is lucky – very fortunate indeed – there comes a second birth, in which the real-seeming self ceases to feel substantial, subject to threat. Who knows why it happens? All the person knows is that the end of suffering is worth the cost of the absence of the old familiar. Even if it feels a bit like you're now a member of a different species.

Only, in fact, your *Homo sapiens* self is still entirely operative. Moving about, needing sleep, nourishment, and quenching. Yes, you will eventually quit, just like all your fellow *Homo sapiens*. Only, you don't dread dying the way you once might have. Not because you assume there to be a disembodied ongoingness, post-death. No, it's just that you're having such a good time being alive.

How can it be that the self came to seem . . . not so serious any-more? No longer worthy of the lifelong fixation on satisfying emotional needs and wants, holding pain at bay, everything a means to one end or another. What made it stop being important that you're thought well of, understood, needed? So strange, after decades of its all mattering so much that to be deprived of respect or security or fulfillment could feel like being radically short on food or breathable air. Why the lightness of heart, without apparent cause, when you used to need things to be a certain way in order to smile, relax, let down your guard? How has it come to this? Instead of being vulnerable to every little thing – people's opinions, change, the world out there, illness and aging – you're okay with each thing as it is; it doesn't matter what. You no longer fight anything. You take it in, as it comes, allow it to register. Then you move on.

Why on God's earth is it so different now? What has happened? The one thing you're pretty sure of is that you didn't cause it. There's one other thing you know for certain: you have never loved this purely in your life. *Pure:* meaning, untainted by fear. Nothing in the heart is holding back anymore.

Oh, you know something awful could come to pass. You know the one you love could cease to be, or the thing you revel in could come apart. Well, everything and everybody does, eventually. You see hard stuff happening around you all the time. Brevity is one of the few things that can be counted upon, your own included.

All you know is, while you're here, while the loved person or activity or condition is shimmeringly alive, nothing in you is tentative. Nothing cowers behind self-protection. The heart is like an enthusiastic little kid, who knows only the now, the juicy luscious now.

When it comes time for the heart to break, it breaks. All the way open. The sorrow has no idea if it will ever end. It doesn't need to know.

Would you rather have been spared this? Would you prefer that the second birth had never occurred?

Are you kidding?

This is how it has been for me, since 2003. At the time of this writing, that's 20 years since the vanquishing of identity. Outer and inner developments over the intervening passage of life have gently yielded ever-deepening clarity. I long ago saw there's no such thing as stability, regarding outer existence or inner.

I have looked back to the before, countless times, trying to see how one thing led to another. I cannot tell. I've pretty much given up the effort, knowing that some things are just not to be gotten hold of. Curiosity unsatisfied is okay just being its curious self. Kind of fun, wondering. Just ask a little kid.

# What Causes Awakening?

There is the compelling (sometimes maddening) question of why awakening happens when it does, and – most gripping – why it *doesn't,* given all the dedicated effort, the intensity of longing. Why does it happen to some and not to others? How we all long to know the answers to these burning questions. Some of us like to think we have the answers. I gradually came to understand only this much: there is no knowing, not with anything remotely approaching certainty.

Of course it's natural to want to know what "works": seekers are perennially searching for a method, something that appears to yield the longed-for outcome.

Why do people wake up, when they do? Some who awaken have never been seekers; others have no idea what's going on inside themselves, and can be deeply unnerved by the abrupt change. Among those who've longed for freedom, some who come to radical clarity don't recognize *this* as the longed-for thing. I count myself among them: it was months before I understood. How can such a thing be? Largely I chalk it up to our tendency (so very familiar, so human, so mind-based) to suppose, ahead of time, that we can have the remotest idea of what it would be like *after.*

It turns out we had no idea at all. It's just as well to acknowledge that, if you're seeking, if you're longing to understand: the mind simply cannot grasp what is altogether beyond its reach. Best to rest from imagining you know anything.

Invite yourself to cease asking *How do I get there?* It's enough simply to get out of your own way. Stop trying so hard, thinking you know what you're doing. Trust yourself to recognize the truth, deep in, when it comes. Discover what it is to be receptive rather than in constant pursuit of the goal. Grow quiet and listen. Hold still. You "know" more than you *think* you do, dear heart – deep knowing and thinking being of distinct orders of reality (the full reality of what it is to be a human being).

A person's turning point – the moment the radical alteration is apparently set in motion – can be registered in the heart or in the body. Or even (are you ready?) *in the mind*. Eckhart Tolle's description of the inner event that changed things for him indicates it was catalyzed by a startling observation of his curious mind. (If you have not read this description, it appears in *The Power of Now*). Nor is Tolle's the only account of a catalyst that was apparently intellect-based.

There are legions of stories about those for whom extreme suffering (with the exhausted surrender that can follow) appears to have precipitated the tipping point.

In my own case, I've mostly stopped trying to sort out what led to things changing the way they did in 2003, and why the radical opening happened when it did. At the time I wrote my first book *(When Fear Falls Away: The Story of a Sudden Awakening)*, I thought I knew precisely when and how the moment of waking up took place. The years have taught me that the truth is likely more complicated than what I supposed at the time. A number of developments (some years before the pivotal event) had occurred in prior life, mostly unrecognized at the time as significant, as "foretelling" an eventual life of radical freedom and peaceful well-being. Learning never ceases.

Nor does opening. Whatever "part" of a given person – mind, heart, body – appears to have been ground zero for the start of things, some who awaken later detect a fuller coming-alive in their other human capacities, components of themselves that had never been free to come radically alive, when the sense-of-self was running the show.

As for me, historically I had been run primarily by my heart and my emotion-soaked mind, relying on the two for a sense of "reality." In the aftermath of the falling away of fear and the arrival of inner stillness (which appears to have happened courtesy of the heart), the primary "blossoming" seemed to occur in my mind – that is, the mind freshly rinsed of thought-driven emotion. No longer at the mercy of desire and identity, this newly-enlivened mind carried nothing of the familiar circular suffering machinery, accustomed to generate mostly angst and useless ideas. This "new" mind was animated by curiosity and awe, with the arrival of occasional insights that came all on their own, unsolicited.

The abrupt clarity in the very organ that had generated vast torment, all my life prior, was (to say the least) startling. Just the same, I knew to trust its insights, since I could sense that the familiar "I" hadn't generated them. Additional developments have occurred over the years since, in heart and in body, as life has continued its unfolding. The result is that I feel more profoundly *alive*, in every sense of what it is to be human, than ever in my entire life.

It's good if a person can stop being surprised by the ongoingness of change, post-awakening. There is no such thing as stability, before awakening or ever after. To suppose there is – whether you're awake or long to be – is to become unnecessarily stuck, to not open beyond where you are.

# What Awakeness is Not

There is a bounty of common assumptions about what it is to awaken, and about what it's like to live in the liberated "state." The vast majority of those impressions are mistaken and therefore misleading. Holding such ideas in the head without questioning their validity (often without even being conscious they're operating) can interfere with the awakening that is trying, in its own way, to occur.

I myself once held many wrong ideas, both before and since waking up. Nor does it appear likely that opening and discovery will ever cease. This applies to each of us, if we remain available to deepening insight. Which is to say *humble:* constantly holding a background recognition of the limits of the mind to fathom what's going on, aware that all things are ceaselessly in flux.

Being awake is not primarily about having certain kinds of experiences. Wakefulness isn't a condition of uninterrupted ecstasy. Yes, phenomena such as bliss and out-of-body experiences may be "symptoms" for some who have become free. These can be second-ary effects of the radical change in the sense of what's real, relating to what "you" are, to what life actually *is,* independent of any ideas about it.

When the sense of reality dramatically alters, it can be a shock to the system. Given the profound shift in the fathoming of real-ity, there may be a loss of bearings. Awakening asks a human be-ing (accustomed to a radically different mode of existing) to make significant adjustments. Each of us is unique in this regard. Things must be allowed to take their natural course. Patience, along with humility, is a blessing.

It's also critical to understand this: these kinds of "altered state" moments can (and often do) occur in a person who is not awake. In fact, the celebrated experiences are not typically indicators that a person has fully awakened, in a stable sense. Are they glimpses, hints, of the larger reality? Who's to say? They may be; they may be otherwise. The point is to not make too much of them, to not indulge in earnest – and fruitless – efforts to cultivate such experiences, to get them to recur, or to last.

Of course they feel good! So much better than the angst familiar to a human being. But to go chasing certain kinds of experience is a waste of life. If you notice yourself taking seriously this kind of pursuit, gently remind yourself this is the desiring mind at work. Being awake is less a particular type of experience than it's simply a mode of being – an orientation to self, to unfolding life.

A common assumption is that when awakening occurs, all of the wisdom of enlightenment arrives on that very day. Although the transformation classically signals the dramatic cessation of familiar torments (mind-caused suffering, attachment, the mistaking of reality for thoughts about it), waking up typically sets in motion a further unfolding. Inner development never ceases. The initial shift is simply the opening of a door that was unable to open before. On the other side of that blessed opening is the possibility of endless revelation and deepening insight – *if, that is, the person does not declare "I have arrived."* Awakening is only the beginning of discovery, most of which could not have occurred when the mind was running the show. There is much to learn!

The fuller truth of realization – what it's like after – is paid insufficient attention by spiritual seekers. This is not surprising, given the prime motivator for seeking awakening in the first place: to stop suffering. All eyes tend to be on the "final" goal, as it promises blessed relief. Yet to assume (or to attempt to impose) anything like stability is to become stuck – to hold at bay the potential blessings of growing clarity.

Even an awake person can get stuck, or can be subject to the forces of enduring humanness. Legendary are the accounts of apparently awake "beings" turning out to be subject to oh-so-human foibles. We do not stop being human when awakening occurs. (Nor, by the way, does the troublesome behavior of a revered teacher, one who's been a blessing in others' lives, necessarily render those blessings invalid.)

How all of this can wreak havoc with the mind of the earnest spiritual seeker.

Not all awake people are alike or experience wakefulness in the same way. Coming to know reality, to be consistently conscious (that is, to not get lost in thought), assumes a wide range of expressions. The variety appears to have at least something to do with who the person has been prior to awakening, which includes the shaping forces of lived life and its conditioning. Nor does "getting there" occur in a particular way. Some who wake up had never been seekers. Many don't comprehend what has happened to them.

Sometimes residual expressions of ego conditioning can linger in the aftermath of the profound shift. While typically many will have dissolved prior to awakening, for some of us, components of the sense of self will persist awhile, typically (though not inevitably) unwinding as life continues to hold a mirror to us.

Seekers can have the natural tendency to generalize from acquaintance with one person's story. Perhaps you've spent time with a given teacher, or have been immersed in particular books describing how-it-is. Maybe you have a direct acquaintance with a person who appears to be awake. However the ideas of the wakeful condition have come about, a person yearning to be free may naturally assume that "this is how it would be for me," or "this must be how it is for anybody." These assumptions may not even be consciously held. Just the same, they can interfere with a person's direct experience of pure consciousness, causing a moment of clarity and well-being to fail to be recognized for the thing it is: because it doesn't look or feel like their imagining of what the "state" is like.

If you notice yourself making some kind of assumption along these lines, recognize it as just another useless thought. Neither take it seriously nor try to make it disappear. So long as you see it for what it is, it won't get in the way of growing clarity.

Awake people themselves can generalize, assuming "my experience must be like everybody else's." I have been subject to this oh-so-human projection, not even aware I was doing it . . . until life, in its ceaseless mercy to open me to the wider truth of things, put in my face the truth: I was assuming another awake person to be just like me, through and through.

There's a common impression that an awake person lives at a remove from regular life. That once clarity takes over, all the familiar human delights – *and sorrows!* – melt into unearthly bliss. There is the associated idea that things that mattered before simply cease to compel.

As with all else to do with awakening, there's a range of what happens to a person's orientation to familiar life "content" (relationships, activities, priorities). Yes, much will likely fall away, since the majority of what's typically compelled a person has to do with its giving life (or self) some perceived value. Obligation and habit have driven so much of daily life, along with fear and attachment. When all of that has ceased to function in the familiar way (or is ceasing, for its unwinding may be gradual), yes, much surely will come undone.

But does this mean you no longer cherish those you truly love? When love ceases to be knotted up with need and fear, cherishing becomes free to blossom most deliciously. Does waking up cause you to lose your appreciation for coffee, the pleasure of the texture of a certain blanket? If anything, sensory pleasures and ordinary delights are enjoyed more than ever. Gone is the familiar tendency to hurry past such things to get to something "more important."

Yes, awake people can be passionate – about many things. We get to keep being people. To have fun! To do work we enjoy. Only now, blessedly relieved of identification and attachment, we're able to participate fully in life in a way that doesn't generate suffering. Because we've stopped taking ourselves (and life) so seriously. We've ceased to undertake something as a means to an end, perhaps to gain others' respect and admiration. Gone is the enduring (crippling!) need to give our lives – *our very selves* – "meaning."

Some seekers suppose that after waking up, a person is so attuned to nonmaterial reality (what gets called "the divine") that they lose all interest in physicality, their own and the realities of the surrounding world. Perhaps this happens for some, but it is in no way inevitable. Ceasing to identify with the body and its condition doesn't mean physicality is no longer experienced or enjoyed; nor does the end of identification render bodily discomfort irrelevant. The dissolving of identification and attachment, of the fear of mortality, means it's at long last possible to *enjoy* being embodied – and to attempt to ease the body, if there are signals of pain or weariness.

One of the most stubborn (and misleading) beliefs about waking up is that desire simply melts away. This is not so. Desire itself never was the actual cause of suffering. As one of Buddhism's noble truths makes clear, the real culprit has been *attachment* to the desired thing. What's fueled that dynamic, throughout our hurt-filled lives, was disliking something about the present moment. We humans look to some idea of what would be "better" as a way to escape present-moment reality. Many defined by their egos cannot fathom the possibility of wanting (or hoping) without attachment being in the picture. They strain – fruitlessly, poignantly – to rid themselves of desire and hope, all the while missing the real point. Yes, it is altogether possible to want without being attached to getting, and also to have without clinging, unable to bear the prospect of one day losing. How delicious it is to learn the delight of desire that has nothing whatever to do with denying reality. This kind of freed-up wanting is not a problem-solver; it is about *the thing itself,* as a means to no end whatever but enjoyment.

Does awakening mean you lose all interest in the world "out there"? You may; you may not. If you wake up, will you still know how you want to vote, in a given election? How vividly do I recall an election of some years ago when I very much hoped a certain candidate would come out on top. I remember tears of appreciation for the man streaming down my face as I waited in a long line for my turn to cast my ballot. What's most vivid about that memory, though, is that I asked myself: *If he should lose, will you have trouble accepting that?* I saw, clear as I could see the head of the person in front of me, that there would be no trouble whatever. For as much as I hoped he would win, I was not attached to his being the victor. I knew I would readily move on to whatever reality had now come into being. Life rinsed of attachment, of hope that imprisons (because it cannot bear the prospect of an alternate outcome), is a great blessing. Talk about freedom!

Life for an awake person does not inevitably carry on at an aloof distance from the ordinary. Some have a growing preference for solitude; that is true of me. The point is that each of us continues, in some sense, to be who we are. Features of our familiar selves are still in evidence.

Now comes the most confounding feature of being awake. Many suppose that after waking up, there is no more pain, that there's only a kind of ceaseless disembodied ecstasy. It's natural to suppose this: for all our lives, we have wanted to be done with suffering. Seeking to end pain – not to know reality – is the prime motivator for most entering the spiritual life. Yet if a person keeps opening into the richness of a human existence no longer defined by thought, what becomes apparent is this: *mind-inflicted suffering is different from the ordinary (inevitable) pain of a human life.* For everything, including beloved things and people – our very lives! – inevitably comes to an end.

We have long equated our thoughts-about-life with life itself – as if they were one and the same. Among the truest blessings of awakening is that life and *thoughts about life* are finally recognized as distinct phenomena. We come to see the difference between mind-inflicted pain and the sort that simply is innate to our humanity.

Yes, we will still feel bodily pain and limitation. Yes, we may "lose our minds," still being subject to the mental and physical deterioration that aging may bring about. Bodies are bodies. They age; they decline; they die.

Above all else, this: the deliciously alive human heart, no longer cramped by fear or belief, will surely break when grief comes. What human life does not bring loss – and with it, grief? What purer form can love assume than the vast sorrow of a broken heart, granted all the space it asks? For when love and need (and fear, need's companion) are no longer all-of-a-piece, as they were before, then when loss comes, there is no recoiling from the profound sorrow. Gone is the familiar hurrying grief to an end, or denying it, because it hurts so much simply to feel it.

And so the very experience that can bring the most exquisite human pain may turn out to yield (so surprising!) life's purest gratitude and savoring. My own recent experience with the death of a loved one has led to this: to the most radical opening of the heart a person can bear. This is what comes of complete surrender to grief. There has been, over the years of my post-awakening experience, no more blessed teacher. Such a revelation! Gratitude that stretches the bounds of what can be contained in a mere body.

And here's the best: when the loved one is *still here,* there is no taking them for granted. No keeping the heart muted, against the prospect of possible loss. No, cherishing is blessedly allowed to take completely over. For something in your oh-so-mortal self knows that nothing lasts forever. So what else is there to do but celebrate – *to live!* – while living is possible? For the opportunity to do so will come to an end.

What could be more sumptuous than at last to be able to stretch to the fullness – heart and mind and body – of our human endowment? If we don't get in the way, this is what happens with the unfolding of awakening. When the mischief-generating mind has at last wound down to stillness, what remains? Life itself: delight, savoring, fully embodied (and fleeting) existence, moment by moment.

And around the edges, the arrival of wisdom and awe, curiosity and marveling. These are the occupations of the clear and unburdened mind, relieved of its lifelong focus on the maintenance of the illusory self.

# The Vastness of the
# Wide-Open Heart

The fully awakened heart knows what it is to love unconditionally. What could be more life-altering than to come to dwell in – to dwell *as* – radically fearless love? Liberated from the familiar human ache to control, to recoil from pain, wide-open consciousness is felt to be boundless.

Acceptance of reality is a profound door-opener. There is no separation between you and whatever you're presently aware of. Consciousness itself is not apart from what it detects: if a thing is real, then perceiving human awareness *is* that reality. The awakened heart unflinchingly takes in what's happening. The processing mind – long prone to deny reality, to recoil from its challenges – is brought to utter quietude.

Nor can the egoic human mind remotely fathom such an experience, focused as it is on orienting to ever-changing reality, busily maintaining the sense of an independent self. What typically occupies us as people is this: where am I *in relation to* this that's happening? But that presupposes there is an *I*, and that it's apart from what's happening to it, or around it. Hence the ceaseless need to sort out how to orient to each thing as it comes along.

The whole thing is exhausting. Awakening mercifully delivers a person from all of it. Talk about deliverance.

Sometimes in a human life, love is confronted with hideous suffering. I once read an account by an awake person of sitting in a theater watching a film about the dropping of the atomic bombs on Japan. Containing footage of the devastation, the movie was unflinching in its close-up portrayal of the nightmare visited upon the victims of the bombings. As the viewer took in (without re-coiling) the images and sounds on the screen, he became aware of something bizarre within himself. The footage seemed to have brought him to a state of ecstasy.

Naturally curious, he mused upon what had happened, and eventually was able to account for the seeming contradiction be-tween the pain he was witnessing and the condition of his interior. What he understood was this: when faced with that extremity of suffering (inflicted by one people upon another!), consciousness is asked to widen to such an unaccustomed extent – to open even beyond its familiar spaciousness – that what becomes primary is not the agony and cruelty being witnessed but the purely accepting love that is "holding" it all.

Unbounded consciousness is experienced as love. This is not the familiar oh-so-human emotion, tainted by need and hunger, associated with comfort and mutuality. Limitless love, while it surely does register in the human heart, is of a particular qual-ity and magnitude. What could be more ecstatic than love taking over so thoroughly that there simply is no other reality? Even as – yes! – the compassionate human self is in the presence of visceral agony. The palpable experience under way is altogether outside the bounds of anything recognizable. Nothing has equipped us to un-derstand. The excellent mind of a human being is incapable of ac-counting for the seeming contradiction.

Long after reading that account, I was to experience a curious commingling of pain and rapture in the setting of severity. The pre-cipitating event took place one night some years ago, teaching me a great deal about the primacy of love. My son had been in a terrible car accident. The emergency room of the community hospital had phoned to say he was en route, via ambulance, to a critical care facility better equipped to address his injuries. The nurse said two additional things: "Your son is seriously injured, but conscious," and then she said this: "Drive carefully." The hospital he was being raced to was nearly two hours south of my home; it was a holiday weekend, the interstate likely to have heavy traffic.

I had been getting into bed when the phone rang, having just completed preparations for an eagerly-anticipated walk with my son that was to occur the following day. Trail map in hand, we would meander together through woods, a familiar trek we both loved, to a glorious waterfall neither of us had seen in years.

It was not to be.

I dressed quickly though not in a panic (as my old self would have been), got into the car, headed south. By the time of that accident, my son had been out from under the ravages of heroin for two years. As I drove, the thought came to me: *He survived heroin.* Had I imagined that made him immortal? Now came this new threat to his life. The irony of it. We know nothing, ever, about what's to befall us and those we cherish.

I drove within the speed limit, attuned to the fast-moving traffic around me. Nor, for the first stretch of the lengthy drive to the hospital, did it occur to me to notice the oddness of my careful driving. At some point the ER nurse's caution revisited me: *Drive carefully.* Why, I wondered, had she said that?

Only then did I become aware of the state I was in, courtesy of the extraordinary circumstances. For the extremity of momentary reality had enfolded me in its tender arms. What was real just now, in this moment-by-moment roll toward the hospital my son had been rushed to? Based on what the nurse had said, I knew he was likely still alive. I also knew that he was badly hurt and probably would require surgery. I was aware I couldn't know more until I arrived and received updates from the trauma department. Lest his addiction be stirred back to life, I would need to alert the caregivers to my son's prior drug use, as they administered necessary opioids. He may have thought to tell them this, but he might not have: he was in shock and in terrible pain.

What else did I "know" – did I *feel* – on the drive toward my crushed son? The vastness of cherishing: that is what overwhelmed all else. Nor did I lose sight of the severity of his situation. This was not denial. Yet somehow during the interval of not-knowing, defined by the miles separating me from the hospital, what obliterated all else was my love for my boy. Even as – yes (talk about miracles!) – I was able to attune sufficiently to the heavy traffic all around my vehicle to take care not to get into an accident myself.

I was in a state of ecstasy. Long after, I'd recall the account of the man watching the film about the atomic bombs. It would shine light on what I'd felt that night en route to the hospital.

Now, heading down the interstate, I understood the kindly nurse's words about driving carefully. She naturally supposed that maternal terror would press hard on the accelerator, possibly putting me at risk. Only then, when I turned attention to my body, did I become aware of the curiously *not pounding* heart.

When I arrived at the emergency room, my daughter was already there. The nurses hadn't yet allowed her in to see her brother. She too was concerned about the risk of his being given opioids. We let a nurse know of his history, urging her to inform the doctors. Then we sat in the waiting room of the trauma unit until we'd be called in to see him. My son's father, having a greater distance to travel, wouldn't arrive for some time.

At last my daughter and I were able to enter the room. My son's face was swollen and bruised so severely from the impact that he was barely recognizable. Though he was terrified and in extreme pain, we could see he was aware we'd come in. His head and neck were in a brace. His sister and I drew chairs to opposite sides of the bed. He couldn't turn to us, speaking only with great difficulty. We stroked his arms, softly said we loved him. We let him know we'd told the nurse of his drug history.

Nothing to do now but wait, to search for comforting words to murmur. Although I could have no idea what was ahead for my son, I was aware there was not a drop of fear in me. Despite his awful physical appearance and palpable discomfort, the overriding thing I felt was love.

Across the circular trauma unit, in a distant room visible through its open door, someone yelled *Code blue!* and began frantic chest compressions. In an instant the space was so full of personnel in white that we no longer could see the person's bed. We never knew the outcome.

There was to be surgery and a lengthy period of recovery for my son, including weeks in a rehab facility (different from the drug sort of rehab long familiar to him). Despite the necessity of pain-killers at the beginning, his addiction mercifully was not re-started. Months would pass before he would walk again. The idea of an uphill hike to the waterfall we'd so looked forward to became a thing of mother-and-son lore, a lesson for both of us: you just never know what's around the corner.

I wouldn't notice this parallel until long after the accident, but the strange calm of that drive to the emergency room had been reminiscent of a long-ago night when I'd been on my way to a different hospital. It was an event that occurred soon after my awakening in 2003. That time, my son had been driven to the local emergency room by his father, who'd phoned me from his house in the middle of the night, suspecting our hallucinating boy to be using drugs. Once upon a time that call would've put me into a panic. Bizarrely, I headed for the hospital without rushing. I remember pausing en route to linger over the gorgeous full moon as it illumined the Connecticut River.

In neither case could the curious sense of well-being be accounted for by my "knowing" everything-would-be-fine. Nor did I – could I ever! – know such a thing. It was simply that love in its purity was flooding all of conscious awareness, obliterating everything else. Unconditional love knows there's no certainty about anything, ever. But what mother can bear to feel such a truth in her bones? Only one who is blessedly liberated from clinging to the illusion of control, who is no longer at the mercy of fear.

People who have lived in concentration camps or experienced life-threatening warfare, who've known any extremity at the brink of life and death, will occasionally observe something curious. An inner quiet descends. Time is felt to stop. This can occur in the context of a serious car accident or some other health emergency. In the profound stillness that may come in such a crisis, a person may later report having never felt so purely *alive*. Even as (yes!) death is staring them in the face. For what could more radically shake a person awake than something like this?

Just when familiar perception registers a thing as an unmitigated nightmare, the person may feel what will later be seen (if they survive) as one of their life's high points. For into that arrested and arresting moment descended a quiet miracle, enabling them to know, perhaps for the first and final time, the blessedness of radical aliveness. What could be more precious than such an experience? And yet to the ordinary mind, more bewildering?

Here's the compelling question: Why does it take a life-altering crisis to bring us to this recognition?

Loving unconditionally, with the full acceptance of reality, is a rare phenomenon. In the case of a love-based relationship, whether between partners or family members, there tends to be discomfort with uncertainty or risk, giving rise to the wish to exert control. Denial runs rampant, with unconscious projection being the norm – all of it in the name of protecting ourselves from pain. But sometimes reality turns out to be painful.

We want to be able to count on stability, and for our affection to be reciprocated. Love, we believe, is meant to fulfill us. Many a relationship is at least as much "about me" as it is about delighting in the other, in letting that person be who they are. The eyes are likely averted from any sign of trouble or change, from evidence to the contrary of what one wishes were the case. Reality can feel threatening, if there's a perceived risk in being truthful, even to oneself. Nor do we welcome the unknowability of what lies ahead. It's a tall order to look in the face of the truth that we cannot assure continuance of a close connection.

The tit-for-tat of love is a deadening force: *I will love you if you love me back, if you promise never to leave or disappoint me.* The dynamic is shot through with delusion, avoidance, and conflict.

Putting conditions on love boxes it in, makes it smaller than it would otherwise be. Instead of being endless space, with fresh air moving softly through it, love becomes a windowless, boxed-in, suffocating cell. There could be no more reliable way to imprison the heart – nor (ironically, most poignantly) to drive a wedge between two people, whether family members or in a couple.

Yet such phenomena, when honestly observed, can in fact become valuable teachers. They shine light on what we're attached to, what we fear. Sometimes, if a person can summon the courage to share such things, revealing their innermost fragile selves, the relationship can become more authentic, leading to trust, to the deepening of the connection. When frankness enters the picture, it might be seen that change is in order. All of this is about the willingness to accept risk, in the name of authenticity – to value truth above stability.

By marked contrast with the airless prison many a relationship becomes ("Promise you will love me always"), in an atmosphere of radical allowing, love is a deliciously wide-open space with a sweet breeze blowing through it. Unconditional love has nothing whatever to do with need. Attaching any condition places confines around the heart, making it smaller than it would otherwise be. Constraining the heart makes *us* smaller, leading us to live less fully than we otherwise might. Oh, but the perceived risk is great indeed. For it means the eyes are wide open to the unpredictable, to the alarming absence of control.

Love without condition is not about me. It's not "about" anything. It's what it is to be deliciously alive. Yet because of the way love tends to be equated with need and fear, the constrained version sadly is the norm. We're naturally afraid of losing the beloved, one way or another, that our feelings will not be reciprocated in kind. The relationship may not deliver what we wish it would. It's all about perceived risk.

Meanwhile, the biggest risk of all is the one most of us willingly (if unconsciously) take: that we will never know the bodied sensation of wide-open love. For to live in unresisting acceptance of reality asks a great deal of a person. Yet the cost of this tradeoff is dear. Just ask someone on their death bed: was it wise, after all, to put constraints on the heart? If they had it to do over, is that how they would live? God save you from that regret, dear heart. Risk be damned!

Nor is it possible to guarantee the well-being of someone dear to us. Where is all of this more keenly felt than in the context of a parent's love for a child? *If you are my child, I need to be able to keep you safe, to assure your happiness and fulfillment.* We may not express this in so many words, but it is surely operating, if perhaps below the level of conscious awareness. What could a father or mother know more desperately than the longing to protect the young one from harm, to guarantee their satisfaction in life? Hence what pain could be more acute than acknowledging the limit of our ability to assure anything at all? In the school of learning about the absence of control, there could be no finer teacher than the crushing love for a child. At some point nearly every parent comes to face the truth that there's a limit to how much love can accomplish. The recognition can terrify a person or land them in profound denial. Sometimes it can open a door.

How humbling it is for a parent to realize that a love imagined to be unconditional has in fact been otherwise. We want a child to "turn out well" not only because we wish them happiness, but in part because we suppose that perceived success reflects favorably on us as mother, as father. How many miserable and frustrated young people have turned out to align – superficially – with the goals of their controlling, projecting parents? Is anyone fooled into mistaking this for authentic fulfillment?

Yet we are able to learn, as parents. Life with an adolescent can be a harsh teacher regarding the limits on our ability to assure well-being. To embody that lesson asks an unnerving orientation to one so beloved: it means relaxing the effort to fully protect, to control. It can be wise to allow a child sufficient autonomy to make valuable mistakes, where that's age-appropriate, even if it's hard for a parent to watch. In the long run, a certain amount of hands-off is a gift to a child. Sometimes it's the only way to learn, to mature.

While it flies in the face of what's commonly believed, genuine love has nothing whatever to do with need, attachment to identity, or avoidance of reality. With one's child (or in any significant relationship), wide-open loving that's free of control – *and yet somehow is absent anxiety* – is a miracle difficult to fathom. No wonder unconditional love is rare. Our parents can be forgiven for having failed to love us as we might have wished. All we need do is look into our own hearts to ask whether we ourselves have managed to love anyone in the *unconditional* way we wish we'd been loved in our youth.

In light of all this, perhaps it was inevitable that human beings would come to associate the divine with boundless love free of condition. Full acceptance untainted by judgment (no matter our "imperfections") is what we ache for all our lives. A god untroubled by our shortcomings, cherishing us no matter how we mess up? What could be more welcome? Of course religions would develop around such a prospect: that life beyond death would be paradise, eternal rest enfolded in the tender arms of purely accepting love.

The curious thing is that we deeply intuit the limits on our ability to guarantee anything, whether for ourselves or for one dear to us. This excruciating truth is the source of lifelong anxiety that nothing seems able to soothe. How odd it is, then, that what's constituted our most profound terror can become the environment of the purest peace. It's actually *relieving* to cease distancing ourselves from what we've secretly known to be the case: that the future simply is unknowable, not to be determined by us. To allow ourselves to rest in the truth of the absence of control is to come at last to dwell in the land of being with reality *as it is*. There, in the context of yielding to perennial uncertainty, the heart is undefended. It is able – at long and delicious last – to know what it is to love without condition, and without need. What could be more radically restful, more alive? Such a relief. But what a surprise!

May it not require the nearness of death to fully open your own heart. The "risk" of wide-open love is much less than the nightmare risk of having not really lived – of having never really loved.

# Religion and Spirituality

A human being blessedly is endowed with a dual capacity: to experience our oh-so-mortal physicality and *simultaneously* to attune, in the stillness of the now, to the timeless reality of which we partake. To be incarnate is to inhabit a body, even as we can detect – very nearly *feel,* in a palpable way – a larger truth enfolding and saturating our temporal existence. This means that in addition to attuning us to the sensory world, the body is the "vehicle" through which we know the timeless now.

Here is what spiritual awakening is about: living a fully human life – brimful of love, death, and (yes!) profound sorrow – all the while being neither defined nor imprisoned by any of it. To partake consciously of our twin endowments is the greatest good fortune imaginable.

Our capacities may seem incompatible and irreconcilable, but they are not. Both are thrillingly real. Only to the ordinary mind (or in reductive religious or spiritual orientations to "reality") do vastness and mortality appear contradictory. Attempting mentally to reconcile the two is a waste of effort, of precious life.

The term *incarnation* classically is used to refer to Jesus Christ. The historical figure was a man. He also is said to have been the son of God. Nor is it delusional – or blasphemous! – for you or me to sense that we too partake of the mystery that gave rise to Christianity. I cannot imagine the historical Christ having wished for us anything sweeter than palpably to *know* the intersection of time and timelessness. Nor is it relevant whether we consider ourselves Christians. None of what Christ was about has remotely to do with a system of belief, which cannot hope to be anything but reductive.

Any religious system, its structures likely infused with ideas and dogma, is a pale and sad diminishment of the underlying reality it points to. Yet most organized religions, most of which involve the existence of a deity, appear to have arisen from a deep intuiting of the larger truth of existence, in many cases thousands of years ago.

A good deal of contemporary spirituality unfortunately is subject to the same phenomenon. A spiritual framework may well shed light on the larger truth of things. Yet many a well-meaning seeker, aching for freedom from suffering, will turn spirituality into a means to an end, rather than simply taking refuge in its wisdom as each moment of life arrives. Perennially keeping the eyes fixed on a desired future looks over the head of *what is,* just now. The desire to awaken thereby (most poignantly) actually interferes with the prospect of coming to know radical peace – to see that "it" is already here, however seldom it may be experienced.

Evidence of this phenomenon is the nondual allergy to the use of the word "I," along with the tortured practice of referring to oneself in the third person ("the character"). What's wrong with having a name, with being a somebody? As if using the correct lingo had anything whatever to do with attuning to reality! It is a colossal squandering of life energy, altogether missing the point, without benefit for one longing to become free of mental constructs and identity. Isn't it clear that the strained effort to say-it-right is the activity of the very mind that's in the way of radical truth? However well intended, it's all misguided and useless.

Yet the underlying wisdom of nonduality – rather like what underlies much religious doctrine – is surely profound. It points to the possibility of being an "I" without its generating torment. When a person is relieved of crippling attachment to the self, cleansed of the familiar identification and belief, inhabiting a human skin can turn out to be delicious. Because none of mortal experience is any longer mistaken for what we *are.*

Isn't that the point, after all? To get to be a person and yet not to be lost in the head? To be liberated from lifelong identification with what life has endowed us with, good or bad? What more could a person wish for?

Although I long ago ceased identifying with its belief systems, the Catholicism of my youth surely did bless me with something that's with me to this day. I'm grateful I managed not to "throw out the baby with the bathwater" when I ceased to Be a Catholic. Sometimes former fundamentalist Christians, having parted ways with the rigid ideology of their youth, will reach out to explore their inner lives. In a kindred way (that baby and the bathwater), I gently encourage them to see if they might not revisit Jesus, sans limiting belief systems.

In the months following my 2003 awakening, one of the more stunning moments of dawning had to do with my finally deeply "getting" Jesus Christ. I was in my car and suddenly had to pull over, lest I plow into another vehicle. I needed stillness just then, to enable the shocking realization to register fully. I could never forget it: I saw – actually *felt,* inside my skin – the truth of that man's existence. I felt how his presence palpably shim-mered – shimmers *still,* to this day – with an aching tenderness. It's the wish that each of us could know what he came to realize in himself: that we all are both human and divine. That there's no contradiction whatever. Blasphemy? Only to a mind imprisoned by dogma. It was all rather a stunner – even a little humorous, in light of Catholicism's (unarticulated) message about its alleged "superiority" to traditional Christianity. Such was the enduring legacy of my early years spent in a Catholic church in Miami. My youthful self had registered, in a bodied way, that there was in fact Something Real going on here.

Whether or not they attend religious services, children often do intuit there's something bigger going on.

# To the Reader

Why have I been so lucky, to feel what I feel – to know, in this radically bodied way, the enormity of the heart? Who can say? (I've given up trying.) But this is not "about me." It's got to do with the mysterious endowment of the human heart.

While typically it's the wish to end suffering that leads a seeker to the spiritual life, that potential blessing is a minor point, in the end. It's the vastness of love that awakening has the potential to deliver you to. For this is the endowment of a human being, born with the capacity to experience what it is to be both divine and embodied. Here's the radical truth of the incarnation: it's potentially available to every single ordinary human being.

How I wish for each person – for you, dear reader – that before your life is over, you will come to know this within yourself. To *know* in the pure way: not with your mind, but with your body. Your blessed heart.

*- Jan Frazier*

# How Not to Read This Book

While it contains descriptions of moments and life passages since awakening, particularly in these most recent years, this book is not a memoir, along the lines of *When Fear Falls Away: The Story of a Sudden Awakening*. The purpose of including such developments here is to portray how post-awakening life is for one person, not to provide a comprehensive account.

Nor is this book meant to be "teacherly" per se. Practical guidance may be found in previous books: *The Freedom of Being: At Ease with What Is; Opening the Door: Jan Frazier Teachings on Awakening*; and *The Great Sweetening: Life After Thought*. In addition, my website, JanFrazierTeachings.com, offers periodic essays supporting seekers' explorations.

Above all other ways this book should not be misread is this: to mistake it for an account of how anyone else's post-awakening life would inevitably be, or "should" be, or has been. My experience is meant to be neither something to aspire to nor a standard by which to measure.

I offer what is here knowing the risks it carries: that what I describe will be misunderstood or dismissed; that people will think what's portrayed here is the "right" way. All of which has held me back for a long time. But at last the wish to bear witness, along with the potential value to others, is winning out over the enduring reluctance.

I have never forgotten what a blessing it was to me, post-awakening, to happen upon the books of Krishnamurti, Franklin Merrell-Wolff, and Eckhart Tolle. How much light each of them shed on my own experience! I will always be grateful to them for helping me understand what was going on inside my oh-so-human self.

# The Beginning

## October 2019

I n my own experience, there's been a bounty of evidence that awakening is not one single shining moment altering everything on the interior, in one fell swoop.

There are many beginnings.

The primary transformation announced itself via the abrupt cessation of fear. This occurred in 2003, when I was 50. While I supposed at the time that the radically altered mode would persist essentially unchanged, before long I was to discover otherwise. Multiple awakenings have occurred. Except in the fundamental way – underlying peace having remained essentially unruffled, conscious awareness persisting – the inner world has been in constant flux over all the years since, yielding abundant further opening and growing clarity. Each "stage" has re-formed the orientation to ongoing life.

Things have never held still on the interior, nor do I expect they will. In the face of ceaseless change and deepening insight, humility has become a constant companion. We humans are only (ever) on the receiving end of wisdom, as it arrives. So long as surrender operates (whether you're awake or not), there is no end of blessings.

In addition to being a likely heart-opener, awakening often gives rise to a more profound wisdom, along with enriching the experience of physicality. It has surely been each of these for me. Nor has radical freedom turned out to be the fabled condition of uninterrupted bliss. For to have a human heart is to love: and to love unconstrained by fear or attachment is also, inevitably, to grieve.

At the time of this writing, I am 69. In all the years since the initial awakening, the single most radically transformative turning point occurred in October 2019. It was acute grief that ignited the vast opening. Sorrow is one of love's potent expressions, and so it can be a mighty opener . . . when unresisted. I could not have dreamed my heart could open farther than it already had. For when fear dissolves, as it abruptly did for me all those years ago, it is love that rushes in. It takes up all the space once occupied by fear, leaving the heart utterly undefended. The enormity of the grief that came sixteen years after the primal change was of a magnitude beyond anything I had previously known.

This is the story of the love for a cat. Although it is no more truly "about a cat" than *Moby-Dick* is fundamentally the story of a whale. It's about the way grief – fully surrendered to – has the power to explode open the heart, beyond whatever its prior bounds may have been. Unresisted sorrow is a doorway to the sweetness of love without limits, and with it, a gratitude beyond fathoming.

This is the story of a love so radically taking over as to render the mind dysfunctional.

—๛—

It was all set in motion by the diagnosis, in 2016, of an incurable disease. My cat would grow steadily sicker. He was sixteen at the time. We had been together all his life. He was dear to me. The diagnosis brought immediate clarity to the shaping of my outer life. Since there could be no predicting the timing of a precipitous decline in his condition, I would cease scheduling any distant retreats, not wanting to end up being far from home when he came to a crisis point. It was best to avoid the potential need to cancel, last-minute, a long-planned event.

In the time remaining, what I wanted most was to spend my days with Tiger. I would be there to drink him in, knowing the space for that was winding down. He was to live longer than the vet predicted, dying in October 2019.

While the initial reason for simplifying my life was to be home when my cat was near death, that motivator ultimately was to hold only minor significance. Allowing love to "run the show" over the course of his remaining years was to carry blessings I could not have imagined possible.

How I reveled in the sweet ease of our leisurely days together, my life much less structured than before. I was grateful to be free to accommodate his momentary whim, as when he indicated a wish to move outside to be in the glorious sun, or to curl up in my lap beside the toasty wood stove. So joyfully would I set aside something I'd anticipated doing just then (catch up on email, do a little cooking) when he seemed to want to be outdoors. I allowed him to set the pace and direction of our movements in the yard. We would linger in the glorious sunshine as long as his heart desired. The inside of the car was one of his favorite places, its seats nicely warmed by the sun on the windows. There we sat together, so many timeless hours, so many sunny days. If I needed to be on the phone, my quiet voice interwove with his contented snores.

Inside the house on a chilly day, I would sit with him beside the wood stove, where he most longed to be. I'd enfold his old body, lifting him onto my lap and cradling him. In another moment he might indicate the desire to have a taste of the avocado his human was just then enjoying, a bit of the sweet corn picked that very morning.

Life grew simpler and simpler. It was love that called the shots: blessing beyond all blessings. I never stopped knowing that time was running out. Yet the sorrow of the background awareness of his brevity and looming death in no way diminished the moment-to-moment cherishing.

But time is always running out, isn't it? Moment to moment, all the years we live. All the while love pulls at us, if only we will pay attention, if only we will yield: love and the urgent reality of *now, now, now.*

As the months unspooled, devotion and cherishing blossomed to a fullness I had not experienced before.

And so, when the time inevitably came, did grief.

—◊◊◊—

Although I was not to understand this until long after, by the time of Tiger's death, my heart's capacity had enlarged significantly beyond its prior condition – prior, that is, to his sickness and the changes set in motion by that. Something happened, over those nearly three years, that re-formed the heart that awakening had delivered me to, so long before. Though as the unfolding occurred, I wasn't noticing: for my attention was on him, not on myself.

In the first days and weeks after I laid his beloved body in the ground, so acute and constant was the awareness of his no longer being in the house that all I could manage was simply to be with the pain of each moment. Many times throughout the day it was as if my heart – the blood-delivering organ – might simply cease functioning. From long experience, I knew there was nothing to do but be with the feeling as it was, as it arrived. One after the other after the excruciating other.

Over the course of those early days, there was also the significant *cognitive* registering of Tiger's absence. The familiar places in the rooms where he kept not being. The food and water dishes he did not lower his face to. The routines no longer relevant in my every-morning, -afternoon, -evening, -overnight. Change, change, change. Goneness. All the *not*-happening. It was as though my ordinary existence were breaking apart, everything disconnecting from everything else.

How to exist? Now, with everything altered?

I began to undertake the practical, outer adjustments to the physical: to undo and launder the blankets where he'd lain, to clean and put away his dishes, the litter box. In some way, these activities helped "get it through my head" that he was gone. Throughout the day I would look out the window at the white stone marker over his grave; when I was outdoors I would squat there, stroke its surface where I'd written his name and dates. I'd mentally revisit the visual, the *tactile,* of his beloved – his *stiffened* – body in the earth just below my feet. I would tamp down once again the softened dirt surrounding and beneath the heavy rock. These are the things we do, in consuming grief, because they are what we *can* do: they help begin to make real the unfathomable.

For how can one so dearly familiar, over such a large tract of lived life, be abruptly so radically absent? So enduringly gone? It matters not whether you've seen it coming. Nothing helps; nothing saves us from the-thing-itself, when it finally arrives. Whether animal or human, or some lifelong mode of being, it takes a sustained stretch of newly-altered life to drive into the skull the new and unwelcome truth.

These developments – the acute grief, the cognitive registering, the household adaptations – began, little by little, to be tenderly contained within a larger, more substantial cherishing. I became aware of the increasing flow (undeniably a *bodied* sensation) of an exquisite joy. Some moments when joy, coupled with gratitude, became nearly unbearable to contain in my mere body. It was as if this new expression of love were trying to break me open, bigger somehow than before. Bit by bit the sweetness of love could be felt to supplant the sorrow of having lost my cat.

There were fleeting moments when it seemed I could sense Tiger's disembodied presence, a kind of ongoingness. What joy surged, then, through my body! Even as I knew I could not really know if he was indeed "here."

Love is not constrained by time, by mortality.

—⁓—

Because cognitive functioning had been reduced to responding to immediate circumstance, to the practical matters of momentary existence, I lost awareness (although I did not notice this was happening) of long-habitual – in some cases, necessary – matters having to do with the maintenance of regular life. I was not to discover this until some weeks after the lapses had been occurring. A significant moment came when something brought to my shocked attention that I had not paid my rent several weeks prior. I'd always consistently delivered my check to the landlord ahead of its due date. It was unimaginable that the day had simply come and gone, unnoticed. At first I thought – surely (though there was no recollection) I did pay it; I must have just forgotten. Certain the entry would appear in my check register, I went to see. Nothing there.

This got my attention. As did several other ordinary things requiring cognitive engagement. Little by little the "data" (as I then understood it) began to accumulate, evidence that my mind had ceased its typical competent functioning. When I would be in outer-life situations asking something of the mind, increasingly I noticed difficulty. What had long been automatic, able to occur with unselfconscious ease and competence, now no longer was. Additionally I became aware that my short-term memory had dwindled to nil.

The more attuned I became to my mental functioning, the more vivid it grew that it was greatly diminished. There was difficulty focusing on anything in any sustained way. I began to notice motor changes as well, such as shakiness in my hands, especially if I was hurrying. Response time was conspicuously more sluggish than before.

As was my custom from all the years of wakefulness, not long after registering the mental losses, I simply accepted my new reality. During moments of clarity, I undertook the accustomed practical approach to adapting. I generated lists I might not be able to produce later, making notes of such things as living circumstances that would need to change. Where would I live? Would someone help care for me? How would I manage financially? What doctor appointments would need to be scheduled to diagnose my condition? Knowing my short-term memory to be unreliable, I made notes and set up other external reminders to keep me on track. When driving was necessary, I took care en route not to think or to listen to music, so that my full attention could be on the road.

I confided in several close friends about the changes I was observing. One of them, wide awake herself, asked whether I thought grief might have something to do with the cognitive issues, suggesting that perhaps there was not, in fact, organic change under way. I considered this, but felt it was not the case, in part because by that time – now some weeks after my cat's death – the crippling sorrow of the early days had softened into a predominance of cherishing. When my awareness was on Tiger, the primary sensation was of love, the grief less acute than before.

I might have taken my friend's suggestion to heart. For then, I discounted it.

—⁓—

Outer life was continuing meanwhile, asking for normal functioning. When alone I was mostly okay, in accustomed equanimity. In social or work situations, however, I could become excruciatingly self-conscious, wondering with growing intensity whether others (long accustomed to my easeful competence and reliability) might be observing the changes. The more acutely aware I became of the need to appear normal, the more self-consciousness gave rise to anxiety.

How strange that was: for although the sensation was familiar from my first 50 years, pre-awakening, there had been no noteworthy episodes of anxiety in all the life since then. Given the prolonged absence of the familiar racing heart, its return felt significant. Alarming, even.

It had my attention. As did the marked diminishment of cognitive capacity.

My primary concern at the time, however – the thing rising above all other matters – had to do with my daughter's planned semester abroad. Not many months hence, she was to travel to the other side of the planet, where she would spend six months. There she would be immersed in the triumphant conclusion to her undergraduate degree. I was thrilled for her, as it was asking of her an unaccustomed courage to travel that far from home. Flying would be new to her, as would being in a foreign country. That she was undertaking such an adventure was cause for great celebration.

I was keenly aware that if she were to detect my inner changes, she would cancel her plans, not wanting to be so far away during a time when her recognizable mother was likely to be "disappearing." We were seeing one another frequently in those days; there would be plenty of opportunity for her to observe troubling indicators of something "off" about me.

My focus continued to be on making practical adjustments and – above all – on concealing my changes from my daughter's attentive eyes and tender heart. I did wish the anxious episodes would abate, or at least ease in intensity. But the more devoted I was to protecting my daughter, over the months leading to her trip abroad, the stronger and more frequent the challenging episodes became.

Heightening the intensity of my concern was the looming week-long train trip she and I were about to take. Our being to-gether 24 hours a day would provide abundant opportunities for her to detect something amiss in her mother.

—ɷ—

For some years by that time, I had become accustomed to the periodic "visitation" of a wise disembodied being who clearly loved me without condition. His tenderness was *palpable*, his knowl-edge of my inner landscape without limit. Everything about me appeared to be available to his awareness. (Though there was no visual impression, the presence did feel like a "he.")

In the weeks following Tiger's death, one day while I was on my daily walk, feeling the stirrings of the now-familiar anxiety, I detected the nearness of my friend. I asked whether he might help me deal with these painful episodes of concern about my daughter detecting my changes.

I felt that soft smile envelop me. The all-knowing presence said (without "saying"), *Only love.* I sensed the vast tenderness in which I was held. There was also his characteristic lightheartedness. It was as if he were conveying something about the relative insignificance of the anxiety that had led to my plea for help. As though the stressful episodes – the cognitive change – were no cause for concern.

What I made of his guidance was this: *When you feel anxiety starting up, redirect your attention from the racing heart to the sensation of love. Rather than focusing on trying to figure out the issue with your daughter, instead dwell on your love for her.* He seemed to indicate that redirecting awareness, at such a moment, would restore the accustomed equanimity. If I gave myself the space to cease trying to sort things out, fretting about our upcoming trip, the uncomfortable machinery inside me would abate.

As ever, he was so carefree, so deeply knowing of my inner world. In light of my acute distress, the simplicity of the guidance might have registered as "dismissive." Even so, given his palpable cherishing of me, it was reassuring.

That was my take-away: redirect attention from the worry to my love for my daughter. The guidance surely did help. In the days after the wise counsel came, each time I felt the anxious machinery start up, as soon as I became aware of it, I invited the gentle command to ring in my consciousness. It was a repeated blessing. Always I was immediately restored to reality, my heart opening wide, the rushing in of the long-familiar cherishing, the gratitude. Radical okayness was restored: for the next stretch of time I'd be fine, the appearance of there being a problem having simply dissolved.

I carried *only love* in my background awareness, taking refuge in it again and again, each time one of those episodes began to overtake me. Whenever I invited cherishing for my daughter to flood my heart, I felt restored, at least for an interval, to accustomed ease.

I felt certain I had understood the meaning of "only love." I was to be reminded – for the thousandth time! – of how wrong the mind can be, anytime it supposes it understands. A string of errors was now following me around, none of which I had yet questioned the truth of. Ongoing life, in its vast generosity, was ultimately to reveal the larger meaning of what my guide had offered that day on my walk.

Meanwhile, I continued the by-now-familiar observations of diminishing cognitive function, carrying on with making practical adaptations and provisions. As before, I interpreted my changes to be organic, to be indications of brain deterioration.

Over the course of that fretful period, intermingled with the awareness that my mind wasn't functioning normally, there were indicators of the familiar ability to *attend* when it counted. I noticed this when engaging with spiritual seekers who'd come in search of guidance. In those encounters I was able to "play with a full deck," to attune deeply, in the long-accustomed way, to what a person was expressing. I offered reflections of potential benefit (although – as historically – there wasn't any sense of "deciding" what to say). Conspicuously absent during those exchanges was the discomfiting self-consciousness. Although generally I would register none of this until the aftermath of the encounter: for during my time with a person, attention was entirely on them, not on myself. I was certainly grateful for those experiences. Still, I didn't recognize the observations as the "illuminers" they might have been, regarding the impression of cognitive decline.

The train trip with my daughter, dreaded for what our time together could give rise to, surprisingly ended up providing its own reassurance regarding my mental capacity. It was clear she was detecting nothing. As one day gave rise to the next, some background awareness was registering that there was, in fact, *nothing* for my daughter to discover. Although (as was my custom) I was so simply *with* her, immersed in each delightful episode as it occurred, that for the most part I didn't even revisit my prior concern. Nor did I linger over why I was oddly seeming "normal."

It was only after we returned from the delightful week together, after saying our fond goodbyes and I was once again home in my accustomed solitude, that the blessed revelation was to occur. It seems that when the time is right for a deep fathoming, it simply arrives, without summoning. It is a dawning: we receive the clarity that descends to our open, appreciative hands.

I was in my car, just a short distance from my house. In the immediate aftermath of the joyous adventure with my daughter, who'd just then headed to her own home, my heart was engaged in revisiting the days with her – all the fun, the museums and people, the meals and music, rich conversations we'd had about one thing and another. Driving along, my first time alone in some days, I allowed my heart to drink in every delicious drop, my eyes brimful with gratitude.

I know the exact place on the road where it occurred, the familiar landscape of distant trees enfolding a field laid open to the sun. Abruptly, so vividly, I got it. Clear as the glistening brook my bodily eyes were drinking in, I saw: *I was not losing my mind.* So overwhelmingly had I come to dwell in the heart, since Tiger's death, that during those intervals of cherishing, everything mental simply receded from accessibility. Rendered utterly irrelevant at such moments, the cognitive faculty was far away, tucked in a small and useless room.

Yes, my mind would be accessible (as it had been, here and there) when a situation required it. Otherwise, the dominant condition – now the default – would be the endless space of love and gratitude, its sweetness *felt,* deliciously palpable, in the oh-so-physical body.

Was I grateful *then?* It seemed that I – that my beating heart, my skin-constrained body – might simply explode. Was I glad not to have lost, after all, the ability to think, when thought could be useful? Surely that. But in the larger context of what was now being fathomed about my "condition," the accessibility of cognitive functioning shrank to radical inconsequence.

Though my eyes had taken in the loveliness of the scene a thousand times before, not once since that day has it looked the same. I cannot roll past that stretch of land, en route to some ordinary place, without the moment of dawning coming full into me.

—∿—

At long and welcome last, I was able to comprehend what had occurred. I saw how over the years of tending my cat through his illness, the circumstances had taken me into their tender arms and brought me more fully alive. Tiger's death had exploded all prior barriers. The crushing grief of his dying opened the door for me to know, in a *bodied* way, the non-distinction between love and its varied manifestations: crushing sorrow, boundless joy, gratitude, whatever came. For grieving – when unresisted – is a mighty force in the land of the heart.

The time of great pain had demanded a surrender nothing in my prior life had summoned. Not that there hadn't been major losses (including deaths) over earlier decades. But now I saw how awakening had paved the way for the intensity of this recent grief: waking up had stopped the fear and resistance that once would have distanced me from pain. I no longer protected my heart.

Now I could see how radically I'd misread the cognitive changes. And how I'd misunderstood the fullness of what was meant by *only love*. The reason I'd supposed I got the meaning of the guidance had to do with the way I'd framed my request for help. I had sought the aid of my guide carrying a mistaken assumption: an underlying certainty about mental deterioration being under way. My "problem" (I supposed) being this: how to cope with the anxiety that was visiting me throughout the day, as I noticed occurrences of an inoperative mind.

I had interpreted "only love" to mean this: *When anxiety visits, redirect your attention to the sensation of love.* As in, attuning to that larger something would ease the uncomfortable anxiety. The fuller meaning of *only love* was now apparent: *This is not dementia, dear heart, that has taken you in its fist. It is love: only love. All of this that you perceive is nothing but the vastness of unbounded love.*

And so it was. When the dawning of clarity finally came, did he ever smile then.

While what I'd requested in moments of distress was some kind of momentary "relief," what was offered in response was of a much larger order. The wise presence wanted me to understand, *to rest fully in,* the truth that my heart had simply opened more, courtesy of grief fully allowed. I needed to register that I was in new-to-me territory. And – most significantly – this was a land extending well beyond the familiar bounds of anything accessible via mental functioning.

*Of course* ordinary cognition would be unavailable, in such immersion! For when there is only heart, only love, anything gotten to via the mind is utterly inconsequential. Useless, inaccessible.

The great lesson in all this was never to assume I understand what's going on. Never to presume to frame a request, to orient in a given way to an apparent "problem," in encounters with my guide. No, just shut up and listen.

At long and delicious last, long after the fact, I got it. Which is the way the sluggish mind works, fathoming a thing only in retrospect. At some point I saw how my mistaken interpretation of the "cognitive loss" had been the actual *generator* of the anxiety. It was (is this familiar, dear reader?) not reality but my unconscious assumption about it that was the real issue. All of it based on the oh-so-human premise that the mind could reliably interpret what was going on.

As life continued, what became gently established as the automatic norm was bodied heart awareness. There I have happily swum, and continue to, until this day. I was to learn, bit by bit, how to "come back," when outer circumstances indicated thinking could be useful.

And my cognitive ability? Clear as a bell. Fabulously competent, when summoned for something requiring the mind. If anything, thinking operates even more efficiently than before this enormous change. Since my preferred mode is to dwell in the spaciousness of the cherishing heart, I engage cognition only when the faculty is truly needed. The forays into mental terrain are kept as brief and efficient as they can possibly be. Otherwise, I remain in the beloved space of the grateful heart.

The experience of embodiment had blossomed well beyond what it had been previously. My cat's sickness and death, and the subsequent grief and surrender, located me in an altogether different place from where I'd been before. All of it wrought a profound reconfiguring. The months of immersion in sorrow and gratitude, the quieting of mental functioning, led me to register – to dwell in – the non-distinction between love and its varied expressions (grief, gratitude, savoring).

All barriers were obliterated, including the familiar dividing lines between the present moment and the past, or between one episode and another of my recollected history. All time had become concurrent, everything being *the now*. History was as much of the present as was the current ache of sorrow. The many years of daily existence with Tiger, all the bounty of rich memory going back to his kittenhood and everything that came after, along with our modes of relating throughout all the changes – every bit of it came fully alive in me, as if occurring *right now*.

There were repeating explosions of cherishing and gratitude for all of it, the sorrow being in no way contradictory or obliterating of the joy. At many moments it became nearly unbearable to be so physically contained in a mere body. I simply could not hold the enormity of it.

Only love indeed. Who knows what might be ahead? Not me, certainly. I'm just going along for the ride. What else is there to do? The learning never ceases. Yes, even after awakening: waking up really is only the beginning. And could I end up, after all, going into *actual* dementia one of these days? Of course I could.

## Prayer

Always, lowering his mouth to something
delectable, his eyes falling shut.
The way one might in prayer,
in homage to what is given.
A gesture of glad receptivity.
It may be succulent blades of grass
in brand-new spring. How his lips
would draw them in, how my eyes
would drink his delight,
as if on my tongue.

It was the small pottery dish
I cupped in my hand this early morning
that brought it back: his tender,
appreciative mouth. How on seeing the little bowl
lowered to just below his chin,
he would bow his head, eyes closed,
put the rosy raspy tongue to the delicacy
his devoted servant had prepared
in the winding-down days, the purest joy
a spoon of crunchy almond butter,
a smear of pale green avocado.

And in the several weeks leading
to the last day, how when we were
out in the sweet world together,
he would pause with his pink pads
on a sun-warmed stone in the dirt driveway,
and put his tongue, eyes shut, to the grit
on the flat rock. Something he needed there
– some mineral? I'd squat beside him
to take in his happiness.

Both of us so happy then.

*April 23, 2020*

# Life Since

## As of 2022

# A New Curriculum

Following the early-2020 revelation of all that had occurred since my cat's death, there came a period of adaptation in the first part of the new year. In the aftermath of the concern about dementia, there was a good deal to learn about how to return to familiar reality when that was needed or desired.

The awakening in 2003 had landed me in the sweet stillness of immediacy, where I have dwelled all the years since. The now has long been felt to be the equivalent of reality itself. What was new in the period following Tiger's death was this: the purity of love had taken over so entirely that cherishing came to define, as a default, the experience of each *now* – sufficient to bring to quietude the customary readily-accessible cognition.

This new way was felt in my bones to be the preferred mode of being. With what pure delight did I relax into the welcoming arms of the savoring heart. And so among the things to be learned was how to minimize the occasions for stepping (as it were) from the beloved default consciousness to having access to the territory of thought. That included the "taking seriously" of structures like time, sequence, and duration. I had to discover how to set aside what had become automatic, inherently most natural now – to hold at a tender distance what briefly must be left behind, to enable normal human functioning for whatever interval it was needed.

For hours at a time, lost in the vastness of the heart, I could lose track of my own hunger. I came to understand the legendary accounts of Ramana Maharshi, who retreated to a cave and needed to be cared for. Ordinary human things, such as the requirement for food, were said to be so remote from Ramana's awareness that he had to be fed by those who tended him.

The French painter Séraphine Louis is described as having walked a "tightrope" between ecstasy and what observers interpreted as mental illness. How well I came to know – to navigate – the tentative orientation to ordinary reality. There was the ongoing challenge to learn how to leave behind the beloved space of the interior in order to rejoin the regular human world, where schedule and life's requirements and others' expectations were the order of the day.

Even with the clear preference to dwell entirely in the sensation of love, I understood that I must discover ways to "come back." There was no denying that I loved being alive. That I wanted this life to go on and on, to continue with the familiar richness of experience with dear ones, the animal delight in the natural world. My body needed caring for – by me. I did not wish to depend on others. I wanted to be able to continue living where I have lived for some years. The mind needed to function sufficient to keep me in touch with practical matters like paying the rent and adapting to the change of seasons.

Day by day I was to discover, via observation and implementation – by "practicing," one might say – how to move consciously and fluidly between modes of being. That is, between what had become my new normal, where all was contained within the cherishing heart, and the outer world of ordinary human existence, the arena requiring mental engagement. Which a good deal of life as a human being asks of us.

I did learn, day upon day. The transition *out* and the return *back in* gradually grew easier, more fluid. I discovered how forays from one to the other were able to happen swiftly and briefly, as the heart (and necessity) requested. I found it was entirely possible not to become lost in the land far from the mind. All of which has been enabled by steady conscious awareness, one of the great blessings of wakefulness.

One of the challenges inherent to writing this book has been the need to move back and forth between *being there* (sufficient to render it as truly as possible) and *describing* it – the writerly (oh so cognitive!) attempt to articulate, to portray. In addition, the mind is required to organize the whole text, to render topics in a logical sequence comprehensible to the reader. For when I "go there," it's so easy to lose all track of context. I must yield to the heart's imperative sufficient to be able to render the experience in words. Yet how readily I lose all track, swiftly lost in the delicious immersion itself. There is no such thing as a book, nor can words hope to compute. Is it any wonder I've held off so long at the attempt? But here I am. Here we are, dear reader, you and I.

As life carried on, a kind of guiding principle evolved: I would enter the realm of thought only when it was truly needed. This was saying a good deal, given that previous turning points (earlier "beginnings"), over the years since the 2003 awakening, had already set in motion a reordering of priorities, a bounty of ways to simplify. This new development meant further simplifying a life long since significantly pared down. Over all the years post-awakening, many things already had been let go, in favor of what-matters-most (life being short).

Even with the renewal of this effort, to minimize the need to think or to "be a regular person," each time one of those was asked of me, there was no challenge in happily making the shift, absent strain. Gladly and with ease was I able to resume that mode, as when spending time with someone dear to me, or writing emails or getting my car inspected. Before long, it all unfolded so naturally, so spontaneously, that for the most part I no longer needed to "attend" the transitions. They simply *happened* as needed, all on their own, seldom requiring conscious effort.

As day led to day, I came to detect a blossoming of physicality, my body seeming to come more fully alive. I had long been joyfully *embodied* (even prior to awakening), enjoying physical exertion and delighting in sensory pleasure. What became conspicuous now was that even *non-physical* phenomena – immersion in beloved music, a beloved person entering my awareness – were vividly palpable on the interior of my body.

At the same time, as the realm of cognition was granted permission to keep at a distance, some familiar traits of embodied existence were less conspicuous than before. These included the sense of locatedness, the customary background mental attunement to a schedule or the daily routine, the linearity of before-and-after, the distinction between prior life and the now. The habitual background awareness of the world "out there" was absent. When there was the need to return to ordinary cognitive functioning – to remember *what-day-it-is,* mentally to revisit the larger world (to plan a trip out to buy groceries and the like) – that transition nevertheless took place readily.

It was crystal clear, as all of this was taking shape, that my days – my life, now – would have two necessary features. One was solitude. Being mostly alone would minimize the need to attend outer reality and to interact with others, enabling the inner life to assume primacy. I also wanted my days to be structured as little as possible. The minimizing of a time-defined "container" – scheduling, commitments, tasks relating to household maintenance – enables a delicious spontaneity, as well as granting the space to linger: because nothing (or very little) is on the docket for the day. Much of my existence has a wondrous limberness. I'm free to move liquidly from one thing to another, or simply to linger, without keeping my eyes on the clock.

The blessed mode of being I was delivered to, courtesy of the grief over my cat's death, is what I have lived in – what I have lived *as* – ever since. What's prominent is the sensation of cherishing, whose vastness can seem to burst the bounds of my physical self. Gratitude now takes up virtually all of the "space" once occupied by cognitive functioning. It's as if love aches to explode all boundaries, including the constraints of enfolding mortal flesh.

# Timeless Moments

Contemplating what the sweetness of freedom might be like, a person longing to awaken may suppose it would mean living at a remove from ordinary experience. That matters of the body, and perhaps even of the heart, would largely be concerns of the past, when the ego was running the show. This belief about wakefulness may not be consciously held, but it may be operative just the same.

Nothing could be farther from the truth. At least, in my own experience. The body is deliciously alive, the heart altogether engaged — as is the mind (when it's needed), blessedly unburdened of ego-maintenance. It's a grand way to occupy a human life. Just because a person no longer identifies with the body — its appearance, health, age — does not mean physicality can't be enjoyed! In fact, once identification has ceased, the door opens to delight not available before, back when the body had egoic significance and was animated by fear.

This deeply felt embodiment occurs, yes, along with attunement to the larger reality. In an ongoing way — whatever the momentary bodily experience may consist of — the vast "something bigger" is felt to be shimmering in the background of awareness. At other times vastness is front and center.

My hope is that by sharing a few vivid particulars from recent life, I might enable the earnest seeker to cultivate a more real sense of "what it's like" (or can be).

—◊—

*Just now the body and consciousness turned the corner from sleep to wakefulness: the registering of* I guess I'm ready to get up, start the day. *In my dark bed I sit up, hear the breathing of the dozing cat curled up at the foot of the bed, on the soft blanket that has comforted both our mammalian bodies through the night. Bending forward to feel for her, my new feline companion, I reach my hands tenderly to stroke her warm fur, to murmur my greeting, my gladness to share my bed with her, to share my life. Sitting back up, I consider my interior, my surroundings: awareness moves gently around the dark room, touching the inside of my rested body. Of my heart. It is as though it were the first time I've felt this fullness of cherishing. How can this recognition of the miracle feel brand new, even as my background recollect-or recognizes it as familiar over decades by now? My heart can only just bear it.* How can this be? *it wonders.* How on God's earth can a human being be so lucky?

*My bladder is talking to me. I rise, feel in the dark for the flashlight beside the bed. It's too soon to turn on the lamp. The nightlight on the distant wall could show me the way to the toilet, but the flashlight enables me to keep attuned to movements of the cat, in case she's detected me getting up and means to accompany me to the bathroom.*

*I sit, feel relief in the release of the body's liquid. Each thing delicious: the sensation of the cool plastic seat, the music of the warm urine joining with the welcoming water beneath. Rising, I return to the room of sleeping, turn on one lamp. Stand on the wood floor, let my eyes move easily around the room to take it in. As if I have not seen it all in a long while, or maybe ever before. Above all, the blessed photographs on walls and on shelves here and there. Each image as if new: my young adult son in a suit at a wedding; my dear friend, now dead some years; my daughter at the rim of the Grand Canyon; the beloved dog, long gone; her good friend, the cat who went to be with her two years ago. I could stand here forever, never even start my day. My eyes now drink in the images of my brother, smiling with the Sunday* New York Times *laid out in his lap; the ancient black-and-white of infant me on my father's lap, his back rounded to make an enfolding cave, his forehead tucked to touch my sleepy head, arms tenderly circling my little body.*

*Each morning it happens this way. Nothing in me has yet visited what-day-it-is, whether anything is scheduled today. The sun will not rise for hours.*

—∿—

*For some time – a few hours, the clock on the wall tells me – I have been up, moving about the still house. Coffee, tending the wood stove, breakfast into the cat's dish, oatmeal into my human bowl, music filling the air. The sky out the window has been altogether black, save perhaps the twinkle of a star in the heavens, some portion of the glowing moon.*

*Just now, though, the first hint of color on the horizon through the trees. Everything stops. I know the sky won't hold still. My eyes drink in the blossoming of rose, the brand new light. As if it has never happened before.*

*It hasn't. This dawn has never existed until right now. No sunrise in the billions of years of the planet has been this very one. Nor will it ever repeat. I cannot bear to miss it. I step out onto the porch, facing the woods, the pond down the hill glistening through the trees. It is all utterly still, and so that is the only way it is possible for me to be in its presence.*

*The view stops me, always. No matter whether I've opened the door with a momentum to go snowshoeing, to collect cord wood, or to walk to the car so I can shop for groceries. Hello, I say, as if we've never encountered one another before. Thank you, I say. It's good to see you. It is so quiet. Maybe there's the melancholy song of a train in the distance, the call of a bird. The scent of the air finding my nostrils, in its transit through the trees, over the earth, is a liquor. I drink and drink. I could not ever get enough.*

*If I have a church, this is it, this view from the porch. This place my house sits, where I live. The place of dwelling, of cherishing.*

*The trees have no awareness of the looker on the porch. Nor do the chickadees, going about their morning business. Do they feel this that I feel? Does something kindred go on within the mortal bodies of my fellow earth dwellers?*

*I turn to see the couch at my back, or what passes for one: an assemblage of cushions covered by faded comforters well past their prime. Some of the stuffing has been harvested by enterprising red squirrels intent on nest-building, the fluff having been carried off to line a cozy home for their newborns.*

*It is here I sat with my sweet old cat, throughout his many chapters. I wonder which of us enjoyed it more, sitting beside one another in companionable stillness. How he loved it when the benign sun entered his dear body, saturating his fur, his bones! The nap overtook him, always. He knew no more profound delight than heat: here, on these cushions, in warm times; in the chilly season, beside the wood stove. He has been dead now for some months. His grave is visible from the couch, where I now sit, alone.*

*Yet he is here just the same. When I linger in this place, I feel how time undoes itself. Nor is the beloved sitting place its mere couch self.*

## Not a Couch

It sits on the porch, facing out.
Place for a body or two to be.
The cushion and back, L-shape
body on it. Unless
your body doesn't fold that way.
Is prone to lie, to curl, nose
tucked. The warm of late day,
how the summer sun is
that certain angle, the place it lands.
The L-shaped mammal beside,
round plate on knees. Something
for her, something for you.
Corn, avocado.

Here's the thing. It's not a couch,
not cushion, pillow, blanket.
It's time, and what happened in time.

When I look, I can't not see
– can't not be – it. You.
Us there. Hearts beating.
Happening now. Still. Ever. No
then and now. No line. No couch.
No dead. No memory. No
sorrow. Breathing
in, out, me, you. Still.

*February 2020*

—⁓—

*I am walking in the woods near my house, a thing I do most days, in all seasons. It's one of the places on the earth dearest to me, where I feel most radically alive. The enfolding trees, animal voices, smells, the movement of air, angles of light. Exhilarating, my body in vigorous motion. It's easy to lose track of what is woods, what is me – where one stops, the other begins. The long-ago health incentive to begin this daily practice opened to this: I do it because I love it. Each step along the trail is dearly familiar to eyes, to weight-bearing foot, to heart. I know each component of it in all seasons: the curve of the trail; the stretches prone to puddle to slick muddiness, in warmth and wet; the downhill sections that tend to icy slipperiness, in winter; the water sources where bear and deer quench their thirst, bowing as if in prayer; the sun-warmed patches, in spring, where snakes rest to let the sun thaw their chilled bodies. When there is snow, my feet wear not sneakers but snowshoes. The snow brings such deep quiet. I hold still, at intervals, to drink in the silence.*

*Here, on these brisk walks through the woods, much comes to me, unbidden: lines from a long-forgotten poem or song; an idea for writing I want to do; a creative solution to a practical problem; a reminder of something I enjoy that I'd forgotten about (a food, a piece of music, a beloved friend). I have not gone looking for these things: they just come, out of the blue.*

*I could die here, so happily. What a lovely place it would be when the time comes for my heart to stop. To curl up and sigh, so grateful.*

*The final sensory input the aroma of soil, the music of creaturely feet moving nearby. The moistness and exhale of their curious noses bending to sniff at me, in the waning moments.*

—◇◇◇—

When my eyes fall on the image of one who is beloved, if I'm able to linger there awhile (lingering being the preference, always), what eyes take in, I enter. I *become*. The flat rectangular likeness of this person, this cat or dog, ceases to be its mere representational self. It is an open window, a door thrown wide open. I have left the room my feet stand in, the physical space my gazing eyes have occupied, a moment before now, and I am – awareness is . . . How can mere words convey what's happening, where and when I exist in this now? For it is another time and place from this one. Not just "memory," not a mentally recollected bit of once-upon-a-lived experience I had with this one I cherish. It is unfolding now, alive now. Not only the in-motion events that occurred long ago: it's not merely the observable things that happened then that come alive in this moment, inside my much older body. It's the radical heart of it all, of the person, the creature. It's the joy, the pure aliveness, that surges into this very present-moment self, surging through my vessels, pumping the 69-year-old muscle in my chest, animating the hereness. It all is happening now.

—◇◇◇—

*There is a black-and-white snapshot of me at seven. I stand smiling in the yard I grew up in. The image is square, curly-edged, features indicative of photographs of the era. It is 1960, Miami. The backdrop is the garage my father is building. He loves tools, fixing, tinkering. It's possible to see past me into the dim shade of the interior, through the framing of the door and window that haven't yet materialized, but soon will. My father is devoted to this task, as to all things of importance to him.*

*I am my father's daughter.*

*I stand tall and earnest in my young pants and shirt, feet together, arms hanging at my sides. I seem to be comfortable in my body, happy to be alive. My nature is already evident by then. Though it is only my much older eyes that observe this.*

*Just now, as my mother lifts the Brownie to her squinted eye and presses down, I have probably set aside some absorbing youthful occupation: playing with the kittens in the grass; sitting on the sun-drenched patio figuring things out; shining a flashlight for Daddy, working on one of his projects inside the garage.*

—⁂—

Time is a strange thing. I keep this photo in my bedroom. It stands on my dresser beside the one of baby me in my father's lap. Another picture there shows my happy young mother and father on their wartime wedding day. He is in his Navy uniform, his bride wearing not a wedding gown but a sailor suit dress. Soon, he will be off again to sea. She cannot know whether he will return.

By now I have outlasted both of my parents; both died younger than I am now. I keep these images of us all where I will see them often, so I don't lose track of brevity. The full-length mirror hanging on a nearby wall reminds me, with great kindness, of my own.

Life moves ceaselessly, the way a river does. Until it no longer does.

—⁂—

*I've just now put on my father's wool shirt from his Navy days. He wasn't a large man, and so it fits me pretty well. It must be 60 years old or more, although only recently did it come into my possession, into my savoring hands. While he wore it over many years, nothing about the shirt appears old or worn. My father was one to take care of his things, to treat gently whatever was under his care. He was the same with people. Always he treated his children with the utmost kindness. From him I learned much about love – not through explicit words so much as by means of his patient and attentive ways.*

*My father cherished his life, brief though it was: he died at 52. The last time I saw him I was eighteen. Yet when I enfold my 69-year-old self with his long-ago shirt, when I lift the dark blue fabric to my nose, he is* here: *he is in the very wool my hands stroke, in these buttons his living fingers maneuvered into their respective holes so long ago. My father is in my heart, my very body.*

*Love does not die.*

—⁂—

Another kind of timeless moment with my father has occurred, here and there, over the years:

*I am in my early thirties, driving on the interstate. I'm moving at high speed over the rural terrain of southern Vermont. There are few other cars. My awareness is on the trees rushing past.*

*Suddenly my father is here. It's more than a decade since he died, since I saw his tender smile. Now I feel* him *– it is palpable – inside my body, my chest, the beating heart within. I am flooded with cherishing:* his *cherishing of me, is what it feels like. So awash in gratitude am I at his sudden presence that I forget, for a moment, to marvel:* How can this be?

*Is this actually happening?*
*Soon enough, I feel him go.*

—⁂—

*Some years later, I wake from a restorative night's sleep, blessedly relieved of a torment I fell asleep awash in. Such pain visits me often. I am a mother now, failing often with my beloved son or daughter: being impatient, wanting something for myself that seems in conflict with mothering.*

*As I lie still, coming to wakefulness, sensing this unaccountable but welcome relief, I remember: my father came to me in my sleep. It was not (was it?) a dream. He came offering wisdom. He reminded me, with such tenderness, of a long-ago moment when I was four years old. I'd been petulant with him, distressed he'd brought me the "wrong" gift, not the one I'd wished for, asked for. All the way from post-war Japan, in a ship across the Pacific, then in our 1939 Chevy driving across the entire United States, my father had brought me a little two-wheel bike instead of a wagon. How he did not judge me, only enfolding me in his arms. The enduring memory of the stab in my little heart:* Had I hurt my kind and patient father? *All my life I'd carried the guilt, one of my very earliest memories.*

*What he had come to teach me, decades after his dying – having never been able to be grandfather to my children – was this:* Dwell on how it was to be taken into my arms, to not be judged, that day you were four. Let go the guilt. Give your children that same gift.

*Never again will I be tormented by the memory of my young petulance. I will be less hard on myself. And things will become easier with my children. My gentle and wise father continues, somehow, to help me grow.*

—⁂—

*I stand before the framed 8 x 10 glossy image of a man in middle age. He is gray-haired, so lovely. It's the picture of one who is deeply contented. He smiles softly at the woman holding the camera lens to her 50-year-old eye. The photograph is the visage of one who cherishes.*

*This man is the love of my life.*

*Although by now our time of occupying the same home has ended, everything he was to me, all those years ago, he is still. What animated my heart the moment I pressed the shutter is palpable right now, my much older feet pausing before the framed photo. A flood of celebration goes out in every direction, enfolding my body – rather the way he once did, his arms gathering me tenderly to his chest.*

*All of it has occurred in the space of a few seconds.*

—⚬—

*I sit beside my beloved (he of the 8 x 10) on the Maine coast, the two of us perched on the rocky promontory at the confluence of the Kennebec and Back Rivers. The smell of salt drenches the air, the Atlantic visible in the near distance. The tide is rolling in, little by little but surely. The pulsing sea water mingles with the fresh, salting it. Here and there erupts the glistening gray head of a seal. The sun warms our faces. Little is said, nor needs to be. Casey sits beside us gazing out, her canine nose drinking it all in. The breeze ruffles her black-and-white fur. Who knows what goes on inside that head?*

*We are all side by side, where we most want to be: this beloved place known as Bald Head. Why would anyone ever wish to be anyplace but here? The three of us come here to camp for days at a time each summer.*

*I have deeply loved several men in my life; more than once I've married. Never before have I loved a man the way I do this one. He and I will never marry, there being no need to.*

*As I write these words, many years after that day, we remain dear to one another, though for some time now we have lived apart. That day at Bald Head, I never could have imagined a time when we would dwell anyplace but with one another.*

*Wrong again.*

*Everything he was, all those years ago, he is now. Spontaneously, in a felt instant, every scrap of it is* here, *contained in me, shimmeringly palpable: what it was to feel his arms around me; his patient fire-building expertise, out beneath the stars; how authentic he was, ceaselessly, inclined to articulate what was within (inconvenient or otherwise). All of it is here in me, this present moment: not subject to the diminishment of the passage of time. Nor is any of it eroded by the eventual change of evolving life, when the option of preferring solitude entered the inner landscape, altering the mode of living.*

*Time is not real. What is real is the now.* This: *sitting on the promontory, watching the tide come in, my heart celebrating a cherished teacher.*

## To Krishnamurti, at the Confluence of Two Rivers

I did not know enough to love you
when you walked this earth.
Only once you were gone did I find you.
When you left, new life was just beginning in this body.
When I look at my son,
I see by how many years
I missed you,
your face.

And so I must love you
the only way left to me: eyes on the water,
light glittering its skin, the wind
ruffling it, my hair. The seam of white foam,
zigzagged where the rivers touch.
Moon illumining the woods last night,
stillness moving over the pine-needle floor.
My man as I lay down beside him in the dark tent.
The dog against me, that sigh, gladness
the length of our bodies,
warm, touching.

Each time the seam melts away,
one flowing into the other,
and the lovely world slips
into these pores, and I pour into its arms
(the pulse not of blood, particular,
the intake not of mere breath),
the sensation is of you.

Oh my beloved,
I did not miss you.
When you left, you left me
the whole world to love.

*2006*

—⋙—

Whether gazing upon a beloved object or photograph, or standing in a physical place dear to me; whether bringing before the mind's savoring eye some cherished moment from my lived past, or sinking into a piece of music, or a loved one swimming into awareness – in one beat of the heart, whatever has been gathered into this moment's attention has become the entire consuming reality of the now. All mental processes are stilled. The heart breaks wide open, obliterating the registering of immediate circumstance, spatial and temporal.

What I struggle to describe here is one of the defining features of daily life in the years since my cat's death.

How a physical object is not a mere thing – not now, since only love came to define existence. Anything dear to me is no longer its familiar "unadorned" self. Since the heart explosions after Tiger's death, it's as though beloved objects and locations have come to contain, within their palpable substance, boundless gratitude. When eyes land there, cherishing is summoned, all in a rush, the heart and body stunned to a stillness that longs only to be here. Nothing to do with time or thought is remotely accessible.

I am surrounded, in my daily living, by a richness of objects dear to me. In recent years I've rid my home of most anything I don't cherish, beyond the necessities supporting ongoing life. As a result, so much available to my drinking-in eyes is a "container": it embodies – *contains* – enormous wealth to the feasting eyes that happen upon it.

It may be a household item, like the mug my daughter made, an image of the two of us on its shiny beveled surface. My ancient rolled-up sleeping bag, happy cozy enfolder of my sleeping self, over so many camping adventures. A photograph (my walls are covered with them) is a potent "evoker." Perhaps a pencil drawing tacked to the wall, some other bit of memorabilia. A printout of a poem from long ago.

I'm merely passing by something or other – on my way downstairs, en route to another room, or heading out to the car, or maybe I'm sitting in my chair – and my eyes fall someplace. I'll see a certain thing, a view out the window, and I'm altogether captured. My body grows utterly still, right where it is. Time stops, and with it, all momentum.

Inevitably, I've had to learn how to leave the timeless moment of savoring in order to "revisit" the surrounding context of my human life. Bit by bit I have discovered how to return to outer reality, to remember there is such a thing as ordinary time – such a thing as a mind, a body. Because I *am* a human being! The house I occupy is beloved and requires a certain amount of tending. Practical life stuff asks for some measure of attention. There *is* a calendar with commitments on it. I want to spend time with people dear to me. The larger world containing all of this is ongoing.

I've cultivated a way to get my bearings, putting a fingertip to physicality, my own and the surrounding. The process of re-attuning begins with registering bodily sensation. Sometimes I discover the presence of hunger, of a bladder asking for attention, for release. I can tell these forces have been tapping me on the shoulder for a while now, patiently waiting. Rather like a devoted dog not wanting to intrude on its adored human.

As the re-attuning to context continues, I broaden awareness from my body's interior to where it's presently located, noticing the immediate scene surrounding me. Then, bit by bit, and with enormous tenderness, I re-enter the realm of practical time. I remember what today is, revisiting what it holds, recalling the season of the year we're in. The excellent mind is handy for such undertakings, ready to spring into action at a moment's notice. Calendars and lists are likewise handy.

Yet only moments before, there was not the remotest awareness of there being such a thing as a mind, so still was it. Now, having "run my hands" over the bigger picture to get the lay-of-the-land, ready to return to the business of ongoing existence, I know that, as the day unfolds, there will be the ceaseless background awareness of the blessed *other*.

I can return there at will.

I smile just now. For as I sit here at the keyboard, working at rendering all of this into words, I become aware that the air around me has grown mighty chilly. *Oh* (the poked-awake mind registers), *it's winter!* I've neglected the wood stove.

—◊—

Much outdoors has the potency to bring my body to this still-ness. Maybe I'm moving around outside, returning from a walk, or about to head out to do errands. Standing beside the car, say, whose door handle I was about to grasp, I'll catch sight of my sweet abode. Or perhaps I'm in the woods, gazing up through the trees along the trail I walk, and my eyes will fall on the house of joy, the place that cradles my daily living. Nothing is possible then but to hold still. To linger, as long as the heart desires. How time stops, arresting any momentum that might, an instant before, have been animating my body. It could be the sight of a hawk soaring above my earth-bound eyes: one lusty downbeat of a magnificent wing obliterates all mind-invented context. For nothing else is real right now but *this*.

Physical engagement with an object can do it. A human being is blessedly endowed with multiple faculties of touch. Hands are one way. There's the shape and texture of a thing cupped by sensi-tive fingers. Or running aging palms over the luscious body of the cat who's recently taken up residence with me. Reaching up to a high shelf to draw down the ancient metal food tray. Its colorful images of whimsical felines have faded with time, over so many episodes of delivering tasty food to a hungry one (including to my own dear self). Eyes too have their way of touching: running over the golden body of my fellow mammal, snoring contentedly beside the fire.

Even this keyboard whose sometimes-sticking keys my fingers presently press into action, so I might share all these things with you. This plastic gadget, endowed with miraculous power to *record:* even the fingered sensation of something ordinary and mechanical like a computer keyboard can manage to cease momentarily the fierce forward motion to *get it down.*

Touch is perfectly delicious. It's a miracle anything ever gets done in my regular-person life. (Never mind that a book might be written to its conclusion.) I've had to cultivate self-discipline when keeping-on-task is in order. So much around me that's visible (touchable!) can draw me in, one irresistible "black hole" giving rise to another, to another. If I allow awareness to yield to the fierce pull, as each time it longs to, I am simply gone from any mind-retrievable context. Pretty soon nothing at all – none of the things I truly want to do – is gotten to.

Just now it occurs to me, with no small measure of whimsy, that what I'm characterizing as one black hole leading to another is rather like what used to happen with egoic thought. The noteworthy difference being that the prior phenomenon generated nothing but misery, while the nowadays version yields only delight and a bounty of savoring.

When something is dear to me, it's because it *contains* associations, stirring beloved memories to life. They're recollections inherent to the thing, the place – actually embodied there. Why keep something at all, in an ever-simplifying existence, if it isn't precious? And then, having held on to it, why hurry past it, the way we do when an object is a fixture of our day-to-day?

My daily living is jam-packed with cherished things, none of which is a mere *thing*. And so how readily do I pause, if only for a moment, to linger – to allow whatever-it-is to take me into its arms and carry me away. If we don't grant ourselves such pleasure, why bother to live? Soon enough death comes.

It's the same with the revisiting of a past experience. Once upon a time, two of my life's purest joys were riding roller coasters and downhill skiing. How I did revel in speed back then.

—⚭—

*Just now, following my dawn meanderings among the wild brush that passes for my "garden," I have paused to check my legs for ticks, lest they use me as a transport vehicle into my house, where I would rather the little critters do not cohabitate with me (or my cat). I hike up the legs of my cozy pajama bottoms to examine my shins for hitchhikers. So that I can see all around the lower leg, I bend my creaky knees, eyes scanning calves and shins.*

*For a few exhilarating seconds, I've lost all track of the prospect of Lyme disease. The posture I've just now assumed is dearly familiar, from decades before: I am back on my downhill skis, twenty-something shins pressing hard into the winter boots clamped to the slender waxed devices, which (even now!) race my rapturous body down the sun-glistening slope. Oh snow, luscious snow! How could anyone not love snow? Even if I'd never ventured onto skis, the longing for snow and mountainous landscape would have been reason aplenty to launch me out of the heat and the flat of South Florida and sail me into New England, when I was a young woman.*

*These flaky bare shins my eyes now range over, checking for ticks in my old-lady driveway, are the very shins that once leaned exultantly into toasty plastic boots, sailing my youthful self down a mountainside on a brisk winter morning. Happy, happy, happy.*

—⚭—

Occasionally somebody hearing me wax rhapsodic about skiing will ask why I don't do it now. After all, I'm pretty fit for an elder. But see, I don't *need* to do it again: I did it! My body has never forgotten. It's effortless for me to go there at will, to re-enter bodily those recollected experiences. When my eyes fall shut into the sight and feel of a long-ago slope, the exhilaration is alive and well. Nor when I return to the present is there any wistfulness. Meanwhile, here I stand, flex-legged in the driveway checking for ticks.

I can ski anytime I want, without spending all the bucks, without subjecting my aging bones to risk. And as for roller coasters, which ask nothing of a person but to sit happily clamped into place on a train of connected cars, occupied by screaming riders hauling ass at breathtaking speed nearly *straight down* the initial drop . . . Well, as a matter of fact, not long ago I did set out to ride the Superman one last time. Yes, I was the oldest person in line, by a lot. Slowed down as I surely am, the thrill of speed has not altogether left my bones. My adult daughter – still a kid herself regarding roller coasters (she is her mother's daughter) – kindly stood beside me, pretending not to notice the scrutiny of the eyes of the much-youngers in line with us. To endure this hours-long line, one must be a true roller coaster devotee. These were "my people," however little *they* might have related to the aging one in their midst.

As it happened (alas), that time on the Superman did not turn out to be the thrill of yore. In the years since I'd last ridden it, my body had changed. The nausea that had never before afflicted me (the threat of which deters many a person from such rides) had taken up residence in my aging gut. At the end of the ride, my loving daughter helped me find the way to a bench; no, I assured her, I didn't need to go to the first-aid clinic. I just needed a wee bit of recovery time. She allowed me to rest my bowling ball head in her lap awhile. As I lay there, feeling my child's tender hand stroke my shoulders and head, it registered: *This was the last time.*

No matter: I knew I'd always be able to ride again at will.

But once upon a very long while ago, I could never get my fill of something reveled in. The impulse for *more-more-more* verged on addiction. Each time on the forlorn drive home from a day on the slopes, or following a rapturous day on that roller coaster, I'd be lamenting it was over, plotting a way to go back as soon as I could manage. *Enough* was not to be fathomed.

And in a sense, that quality of my familiar greedy self endures to this day: though its expression differs. Now, it's purely, simply, *life itself* that I want more and more of. I couldn't ever get my fill of living. For it's not the "contents" of a day, of a moment: it's life itself. It's the bodied sensation of aliveness.

Here's what's different from before. I'm well aware that were it all to come to an abrupt stop (as one day it surely will), nothing in me would lament or feel regret. I would – I will – gladly relax into the arms of the inevitable. Because I have lived, really lived. Having at long last learned not to squander the precious moment, I experience each now as altogether delicious, capable of filling me to the brim. Whatever it may hold.

It never was, you see, about life's "content": it's about the presence that registers it. It's got to do with the conscious awareness holding the fleeting now – the way ski boots once enfolded my legs, the way the roller-coaster seat held my screaming self.

Nor is there any contradiction between the two: on the one hand, a given moment being the definition of *plenty;* on the other, hoping life goes on and on. How can it be, that these two things co-exist? But they do. Nor is it possible to imagine a good fortune to exceed this one.

—⁓—

If something practical needs doing just now, what's in order is gently to resist the draw toward a would-be rabbit hole. It may be a photograph, a piece of music, a scent on the air – anything holding the power to capture awareness, plunging me into timelessness. This dynamic carries on all day long. Since much that the senses detect holds this magnetic pull, I've had to learn to rein myself in. It's a newly-acquired skill.

And if "real life" *doesn't* need attention just now (and I've simplified my days to minimize that), when something takes hold of attention, I yield joyfully. Gladly – so gladly – does the brimming heart give way to the welcoming. Never do I feel more radically alive than at such a moment.

I hold altogether still. There's no inclination to withdraw attention from where it is – to move, whether outwardly or within. Indeed, were I to attempt to set my body in motion just then, it first would be necessary to "revisit" my immediate location, to get my physical bearings.

All context – what today is, the larger world, what time of year it is, things planned for the day ahead – has melted away. Any sense of linearity and sequence (the meaning of before or after, of duration) is simply absent. The familiar distinction between past and present, between recent and long ago, between physically-here and not-here, has no felt meaning.

Rapture takes completely over. At times the bodied sensation is so overwhelming as to strain flesh-bound physicality. It's almost as if I cannot get large enough to hold the cherishing of what is, of what has been. As if my mortal body is aching to explode its limits.

Nor is there any inclination for this to be otherwise. Since the time of my cat's dying, the commanding preference of my everyday is to dwell in the heart. Nothing can hope to compete with it.

An image of my friend Mary hangs in my living room. Each time I pause to drink in her beloved face, so much comes alive.

—⁂—

*We are moving slowly among the redwoods. Mary has brought me to this place I have longed all my life to be. We seem to be the only ones here just now, moving among the wordless giants. Seldom does either of us speak, and then only a whispered word or two. What could want saying, in the presence of such profound silence, such grandeur and beauty? Later, she'll say our time in the trees was reminiscent of being in church. Neither of us has been inside one of those in ages. But now, here, what is either of us experiencing but worship?*

—m—

The walk among the redwoods took place many years ago, but in this moment, I can feel us there. By now Mary has been dead a long while; she was 20 years my elder. I miss her. Every now and again I can sense her loving presence.

One of my life's truest friends, Mary was an enduring soulmate over many chapters. In the weeks after my awakening, she was one of the few I struggled to tell of what was happening. I will never forget that day. We walked among different trees on that occasion, the woods trail meandering through a park in Massachusetts, where each of us lived in that era. How patiently she attended my halting words, the long silences between.

Not many of my relationships were to survive that profound turning point in my life. For I seemed to be no longer the person I had been. With one another though, Mary and I were the same as we'd always been: in full acceptance of one another, whatever change might come, whatever the moment may hold.

—m—

The music filling the air just now is Gabriel Fauré's *Pie Jesu*. The Fauré *Requiem* entered my life when I was in my late teens, singing alto in a choir. Ever after the piece would live in me. Such beauty, a rapturous portrait of death, of after.

Some years ago I attended a performance of the *Requiem*. I went alone, needing no company but the glorious music. I happened upon a writing friend – a kindred spirit, in two regards: she too loved the piece, and she also had no need of society. We took seats beside one another, no need to chat. When the lights went down and the opening notes filled the dark room, we lost all awareness of one another. There was only the music. Maybe two or three times, between movements, our eyes found one another's in the semi-dark.

Not long after, I learned she was terminally ill. I was not to see her again. At the memorial service, a soprano sang Fauré's *Pie Jesu*. What else could it possibly have been? Anyone close to Cielle knew how dearly she loved the *Requiem*.

Had she known that day that she was near her end? It's hard to imagine otherwise.

Now when Fauré fills my rooms, saturating the heart of me, I am in that dark auditorium beside Cielle. This is not memory, not a mentally-revisited experience. No: I am there now, with my friend, in a kindred rapture we can only just bear.

—⁂—

*Oh this song . . . the one playing right now, filling my grateful heart. In an instant I am not merely inside the house. I'm sitting with my daughter at the picnic table out in the sun. It's a warm day. The windless sky rises above and all around us and our Scrabble game, splayed on the wooden boards between us. I lift my face to the puffy clouds so high in the endless blue, the soaring hawk sweeping over our heads, calling out.*

*My present-moment eyes gaze out the window, down the hill where the picnic table sits in another season, empty now. Still, the two of us are there, and ever will be, on that timeless long-ago day.*

*My generous daughter has just now been searching on her smart phone for songs to play for her mother, who's recently discovered a delight in Celtic music. Into the sweet summer air of our togetherness comes a tune whose opening notes arrest me. Everything stops: the tune enters my body, lifts me into the sky. In an instant I can only just bear the beauty. It's as though my entire life of loving music has been pa-*

*tiently waiting for* this: *this song (yes), but also for its arrival into this moment – here, now, with my beloved child and her vast heart, the benign rays of the sun blessing us. So that this rapturous music could fill the world, us together in it, ever after.*

*Of course it would come to dwell in my body – the song, that moment in the sun, playing Scrabble with my daughter. Now so long ago, it seems to the curious mind, the recollecting mind of a mother.*

*Now, hearing the song as it fills my living space, months after that summer day, I linger in the single sustained note that comes near the conclusion. It seems to be the moment where all the prior melody has been headed. How that pleading note does pierce me! The piece was written this way so the breakable human heart can land there, so it may linger in sorrow – the breaking heart of what it is to be human. All the poignant aching of the world is contained in this song. The lingering of that held note grants the space for a pause, the room a person needs (longs for!) to break tenderly open all the way.*

*The solitary held note of the uilleann pipes is the very embodiment of lament. Such poignance! After a time I will learn that the name of the song has "lament" as its opening word:* Caoineadh Cú Chulainn. *No wonder the music touches the heart. No wonder it lives in me as it does.*

*For no moment lasts, does it? Except in the timeless space of cherishing.*

*Each time I hear the song, all of this unfolds inside the maternal heart.*

---

What it is about music? How effortlessly its beauty draws me into the extraordinary realm where all life co-exists. Why does music affect me as it does? Whatever it so exquisitely stirs on my interior, music – above all, something carrying particular associations from my decades of living – carries a potency few things do. Nor is it only long-familiar pieces having the power to surge my heart wide open. Something new and arresting (that Celtic song!) will do it.

When I enter certain music, as I feel the notes enter my body, it's as though something dwelling at the heart of reality has opened its welcoming arms to me. "I" am simply gone: what is real, just now, is not me-hearing-the-song, but the song itself. How well T.S. Eliot portrays this in his *Four Quartets:*

> . . . *music heard so deeply*
> *That it is not heard at all, but you are the music*
> *While the music lasts.*

If a given piece does carry associations from lived experience, a particular interval of notes can have the power to put me – body and soul – *right back into that time.* This is not the mind tapping into memory in that ordinary story-revisiting way, the mode long familiar from decades of "living in the past."

Nor are such bits of personal history all feel-good snippets of my long-ago self. Plenty are heartbreaking in their revisiting of acute pain. It's as though the losses, the moments of anguish, were occurring *right now,* the sorrow newly alive in my heart.

That's the way it is each time I play the soundtrack of Leonard Bernstein's *On the Waterfront,* especially a particular passage. It's the quiet opening notes of one song, an achingly beautiful stretch of solitary woodwind and strings. I cannot hear those notes without being brought to utter stillness. For I am back there, right now, in that agonizing moment of early motherhood when it appeared I might have breast cancer. I was a nursing mother. The very part of me sustaining my baby's life, helping his tiny self to grow, could contain the seed of my early demise. How I loved my little boy, born not long before that worrisome mammogram. The idea that I might not live to see him grow – that he might carry no conscious memory of his mama – brought the most acute pain.

Yet Bernstein's music fills my much-older body with not a drop of sorrow. And it isn't because it turned out I didn't have cancer. No: what surges through my skin and bones is how much I loved being alive, being a mother! Feeling the little guy pull ferociously at my nipple, drinking in his tiny face, I wanted desperately to carry on with him.

No matter whether it's playing audibly or simply inside my physical self, music is a huge part of my daily experience. Sometimes on first waking, I'm aware a piece has been playing inside me during sleep. It ushers me into the brand new day.

Among the high points of my rich life of song have been experiences of performing in choruses. That time of hearing the Fauré *Requiem,* sitting beside my friend who was dying, one of the things coming alive inside my heart was the bodied recollection of what it was, decades prior, to stand on a riser and sing that very music. My youthful eyes were riveted on the face and hands of the conductor, who was in a rapture. How his own eyes fell shut through a passage of exquisite beauty. Paul taught the teenaged me as much about love and surrender as he did about music. As if there were a difference! Although he has been dead many years now, I cannot hear the *Requiem* without celebrating for the thousandth time the world Paul opened to me. As the music fills the air, my old lids lower: I am back there once again, in the body of the girl I was, singing my heart out, tears pouring down my face. Paul is alive.

Not long after singing the Fauré, I stood on risers before a different conductor, this time performing Beethoven's *Ninth.* No choral experience has rivaled that one. When I listen now to the fourth movement, as the opening notes of the *Ode to Joy* begin, I can only just bear to take them in. I am back in that long-ago auditorium in Miami, an almost-woman of nineteen in the alto section. I'm in such ecstasy that I can barely manage to make audible the oh-so-soft passage (and for an alto, high!) approaching the climax of the piece, as I struggle furiously to hold tears at bay.

None of this is mere memory. The long-ago experience of singing is visceral, palpably occurring *in this moment*. Every felt bit of it registers in my 69-year-old body. I could happily do nothing else at all, for the rest of my days: just this.

There's another kind of music, the sort generated not by gifted mammals like Mozart, Beethoven, Fauré, and Brahms, but what issues forth from the throats of winged creatures, courtesy of evolution. Oh, birds sing not for the savoring pleasure of we who drink in the beauty. The song of the veery, for instance, one of the dearest musical intervals to my human ears. Like all birds, the veery sings not to rejoice, to show off its gifts, but merely to communicate: to warn away intruders, attract mates, broadcast intelligence of a food source.

But we who revel in symphony, who celebrate the great composers – we cannot help but hold still for the music of the veery and its kin, when it makes its way to our ears. Nor need we know the name of the singer, nor even what the songster looks like. The music is itself: it does what it does to the ecstatic human heart.

—◊—

*Standing in my dining room, close to the back side of the kitchen island where food preparation happens, is a tall-legged stool. It's the sort of thing designed to pull up to a breakfast nook. There's nothing remotely lovely about this piece of furniture: plastic seat of ugly brown, silver legs wobbly and tarnished from the years, seldom dusted. As the world reckons such things, the stool is of no value. Most people would have parted with it long ago. But to my savoring eyes, it is a treasure. Sometimes I pause in the morning's occupation, captured anew by the sight of it. Nothing to do now but run my palm over the hard split plastic. To enter once more (as if she were physically here) the sight and the bodied deliciousness of my grown-up daughter perched there.*

*A crossword puzzle book may be splayed across her lap, her voice calling out clues while I stand on the opposite side of the counter, chopping vegetables. Or the guitar may be propped on her thighs, the fingers of one hand fretting a chord, the nails of the other picking, strumming. Her cozy slippers are propped on the metal ring below the seat. Maybe she's singing; perhaps I am too, if it's one I know. Most likely, I hum along softly, so I can drink in the sound of her voice. So I can memorize it, you might say: for she won't always be here.*

*In the present-tense moment, when it's not my daughter but my own recollecting hand caressing the seat, her voice even so fills the room we both joyfully inhabit. For she is as happy to be here as her mother is to have her. My daughter's physicality is no more palpable when we're breathing the same air than it is in this now, with me alone in the house, remembering. The room is alive with companionable laughter, with song, talk, puzzle-solving – the music of mother and daughter alive in a common moment. Every scrap of it is right now. Though the stool does not presently hold her, she is* here, *perched on it, her mammal heat softening its tough plastic.*

*If she never sits here again, always will she be on this stool.*

—◆—

*In my car now, rolling over cherished terrain, over long-familiar roads. It's been a while since I've seen Dummerston, my life having simplified a good deal in recent times. Apart from coming here to get the annual fresh-cut Christmas tree, there's seldom reason to travel these roads nowadays. This is a town I once had frequent occasion to drive through, to spend time in. I held writing workshops here; my partner's beloved daughter used to live in Dummerston. So many places I'm driving by bring the past alive in me. It feels a bit like coming home – reminders of eras and people dear to me, some of whom still live here. Though they (we all) are a good bit older now. I keep wanting to stop – to let the car linger, in a quiet stretch of road. I could do that. It's a rural town, slow-moving.*

*At the top of a hill I come to the old church. There is a stop sign. I can hold still for a bit, look. Revisit. For some years I attended a winter solstice ceremony inside there. Candles – the room otherwise dark – glowed from huge evergreens at the two sides of the altar. Mostly, people sat in reverent and blessed silence: the stillness was a welcome respite from the boisterous merriment and commerce of the holiday season. At intervals, a harpist and cellist on the altar played lovely, contemplative music. After, the congregation sang a little, softly, a capella. It was not a chatty event, although as people entered and left, there were quiet exchanges of greeting: nods of recognition, smiles, soft hellos.*

*As I sit gazing at the church through the windshield, it's as if I'm running my hands over the stone building, over the long-ago delicious moments inside there. Like I'm inside the place: right now, sitting on a wooden pew, a kindly stranger to each side of me. We are aware of one another; it's enough. Peace and gratitude permeate the room.*

*No matter that the once-annual event hasn't been held these recent Covid years. Or that this moment at the stop sign is taking place not on the solstice but in early fall. It is all happening now.*

Now: *inside my body, my savoring heart.*

—ɷ—

There is a framed enlargement of my son and his partner, she who is manifestly the love of his life. His shot-through-with-pain life. Such is the lot of one endowed with his vast intelligence and heart. So tenderly does he cradle his beloved in this image, long arm encircling her shoulders, holding her close. In the fullness of time they found one another, following sustained stretches of difficulty in their respective adulthoods. Blessing of blessings: readiness being all.

I sensed early on in my boy's youth a kindred make-up between us, mother and son alike endowed with potent capacities for beauty and (in equal measure) sorrow. A grandeur rode around inside the little guy. I saw myself in his penetrating blue eyes: I too had been that way since childhood. I detected in my son's heart an attunement to the larger truth of things, along with an aching authenticity: he would not be able to be otherwise, even when "the world" asked something different of him.

85

Hence our enduring closeness, throughout all his life's unfolding chapters. We had twin capacities for rapture and for pain. How one quality, in our human kind, does seem to come inevitably with the other! And why, one wonders, did my inner makeup ultimately open to profound ease? Whereas in my son's case there grew the predominance of agony – and so, inevitably, the compelling need for relief, destructive or otherwise.

My eyes linger over the photograph. My heart is flooded, for the ten thousandth time, by the ache of the years of heroin, when his heart could have stopped many moments each day but mercifully did not. Readiness, yes. For he had said to me – so patiently, with such wisdom and kindness – that he knew I was right but could not stop until he knew the time had come.

It came.

—⁓—

*I am sitting on the porch with my son beside me. Things just now have grown quite still. We sit together in a companionable silence, a comfort familiar over our years of knowing one another, through all his passages and my own.*

*It's a lovely day in October, the month of his birth. The colors have begun coming to the leaves. The air is cool, sweet and refreshing. We've been talking for a time, sitting side by side on the couch, gazing out at the trees. Now I notice he has grown quiet.*

*How does he say it? With what tentative words does he begin? For he means me to know that he has parted ways with the life-threatening addiction. For real. As he will haltingly express, long pauses between the words, this has been the case now for some months. Yet he knew not to rush to tell me: for after the years of lying and stealing, of distorting every truth for the sake of the next fix, he realized it would be too much to ask for me to trust the authenticity of what he wanted so much for me to know. Such is the tyranny of the mistress heroin, to which all else – love itself! – must kneel in piteous obeisance. What right had he to suppose I could believe him this time?*

*And so, over these blessed months of coming-back-to-life, he has patiently awaited the right moment to open the door to that revelation. He saw it had arrived.*

*I listen to him tell how it came about. How the fabled "hitting bottom" occurred. The shuddering truth that landed, that moment early in a spring morning following a torturous night. The night had contained no sleep – only the moment of finding himself on the awful verge of punching a fellow addict, his girlfriend then. He describes how time simply stopped. He turned his eyes from the face he was about to punch and looked directly at himself:* at what he had come to.

*As he speaks of that moment of reckoning, I pivot on the couch to look at him. He tells of that dawning. How he walked resolutely out the door and began striding, in the early morning light, in the direction of the nearby hospital – the very place, as it happened, that I had given birth to him. He thought the caregivers in the emergency room could help him take the next necessary step to break free, once and for all, of heroin. He describes how the quickening pace of his feet filled him with exhilaration as he moved toward help. As he registered* I'm alive!

*I watch my son's dear, dear face – the face of my firstborn child – and listen to the words come tenderly from his halting lips. How he hopes so much I can accept the truth of what he is saying. His kind and wise eyes, so very blue, brim with the knowing that I have every right, from long experience, to doubt the authenticity of what he struggles to share.*

*But nothing in me doubts. I see he knows the truth of what he is saying. And so I know it to be the case.*

*The embrace goes on a long while. Who's to say where time disappears to, at such a moment? Such a turning point in a life – in two lives!*

*Over all the years of my son's tortured youth, the era of lies and police cars, of terrible risk and anger, his life constantly in peril, whenever I would offer advice, try to "save" my boy, he would always say, with such clarity and startling maturity:* Mom, I know you're right.

It's just that until I get to where I can see it that way myself, I can't do it.

*Sure enough.*

*When our time together comes to an end, that afternoon of his revelation, I cannot hold still. There's nothing to do but set forth walking down the road I live on. To allow the thing to register, over and over again. My feet, moving with ever-growing speed, begin to feel as though they will lift me right off the dirt surface – that these maternal arms will transform to wings and lift me clear above the trees, high into the glorious blue above me.*

*When in my life have I ever known such boundless gratitude?*

*The trees are the same brilliant colors that filled the sky the morning of my son's birth – his* first *birth, I now see. That long-ago dawn I rushed to the same emergency room, my baby's life in possible peril, due to his position in the uterus. But it turned out my little boy was fine. Oh, so very fine.*

—⁓—

Although many years have passed now since the day of my son's porch revelation, that day continues to live in me, an enduring part of my aging body. The memory will be here when it comes time to slip from this life.

Then we entered a precious stretch of months, of years – the lingering aftermath in which we swam together, mother and son. Such celebration: he was alive again! So many meandering walks in the woods, along rivers; the odyssey to northern California; sunny days of camping in Vermont with his sweet basset hound. Each place the setting for endlessly rich talks – beside a fire, along wooded trails we'd explored in his boyhood, riding together up the Pacific Coast Highway, moving slowly among the profound stillness of the redwoods. Alive, alive!

You see, there's more than one way a life can have a second birth. There's not just one kind of death. There's the sort that explodes open the heart (as happened with me), while the other threatens to stop it altogether.

One of my life's purest miracles is that my son survived. Survives! We have a depth of connection few mother-sons ever manage. It's been that way between us since he was a small boy – and somehow continued, even when his beloved was heroin.

Now here he is, in this photograph I stand before, with she who cherishes him. When I stand here, into my grateful heart swims all of my son's history. We don't see each other nearly as much these days. He has a life now: what could be sweeter? I could wish nothing better for him. Though I miss seeing him as often as I once did, I am not greedy. The past we have shared is (can you see?) present.

I muse, sometimes, about the way my delight in ordinary life leads me to hope I have years and maybe decades left in me. Then something whispers *Yes, and if your wish is granted for more-more-more, do you realize what could be the hideous cost of a lengthy life?* How into the midst of continuance could land the demise of my son, my daughter?

Here it is, the cost of loving without limit, sans protection. We simply don't get the one without the other.

—⁂—

*That photograph of the Grand Canyon, made via a lens lifted to my time-bound face. The view drunk in with dying eyes. How in the bodied presence of the unfathomable, anything to do with time was, in one beat of the heart, crushed to oblivion. That is what being there did. What being there* does: *for I am there now.*

*Space, more space, more, giving way to endlessness, to no-end. Nuanced and gaudy crayon colors shape the canyon, eons of rock giving angle, pitch, bottomlessness. Patience embodied in the vista: no matter how long it would all take. Millennia of creatures roaming, feasting, resting, rotting.*

*The soaring condor absent awe, here in its familiar: it knows nothing else. My heart takes wing with the creature, lifts from the solid where my ungainly arches perch. I have always ached for hollow bones in my arms.*

*If this could be what it is to slip from this skin – spread vast arcing feathers and go, go, current buoying my chest . . .*

*The mind struggles to register: my body is not* now *there, in the glory shimmering from this flat and framed 8 x 10.*

*Oh, but it is.*

*A photo being not mere image. On sight, the image explodes.* There *I am. Forever* here.

—☽—

The experience of profound heart-opening, the dissolving of boundaries, makes vivid the co-existence of present and past. Prior life continues to animate the human heart. This bodied "memory" is markedly different from the mental rehashing of an earlier time. The storied container of recollected history is a kind of static object that exists in the head. It's distorted by interpretation and sculpted by a sense of identity, maintaining the ongoing illusion of a self.

Pieces of the past that dwell in the heart, rinsed of crippling *meaning,* are another matter altogether. Nor does a present-moment revisiting of earlier experience necessarily constitute "living in the past." It can more accurately be said that the past lives in us. It is, after all, the accumulated bounty of our experience that's made each of us into what we are (whether or not it's all "retrievable" via ordinary recollection).

Consciously entering a moment of one's history in a bodied way (not in the head) – palpably sensing the reality of the past's on-goingness, right now – is akin to the discovery of a new dimension. It's as if one previously has known only two dimensionality, having features of just left and right, ahead and behind. Now, abruptly, the present is endowed with three dimensions, where up-and-down has been added to the prior experience of flatness.

Here's another way of looking at it. In what has been called the fourth dimension, all of time is said to co-exist. The explosion of cherishing lands us in the space where all our personal history is concurrent, with the past "contained" in the present. Whatever has been experienced, whatever continues to dwell in the heart (independent of a mental accounting), is still real. The re-*collected* experience is palpable in the body, in this moment.

These are the words of T.S. Eliot:

> *Time present and time past*
> *Are both perhaps present in time future.*

The poet is saying that in some sense, all of time co-exists. Each moment of a person's lived life *is* the present, contained in immediacy. It continues to animate us now, the sweet and the sorrow of whatever has occurred. No matter whether it's been grieved or celebrated, learned from or disregarded, consciously recollected or forgotten, or suppressed.

Nor can the mind hope to understand how this can be; any attempt to do so is inevitably reductive. This is not about ordinary memory; it has nothing whatever to do with the interpreting mind. Yet something in the alive human body – the same *something* able to register momentary aliveness – knows the truth of it. Whatever has shaped each of us into what we are is alive within us until we die.

# Knowing

There is more than one way that *knowing* takes place in a human being. This is the case whether or not a person is awake. For the most part the occurrence of a given episode of knowing, when it's under way, is not observed. Nor do most of us commonly associate the two breeds of intelligence, or recognize them as being kindred, and alike innate to our humanness.

Only in recent life has all of this sorted itself out in my observing consciousness. Though since awakening, I have been vividly aware of both types of intelligence operating, appreciating the potency of each.

One way of knowing is experienced somewhat physically, in the body. It is *felt*, palpable. Such a moment tends to arrive spontaneously, unbidden. It may be startling. If you allow yourself to pause, you will notice that all momentum, including anything mental, has grown quiet. This intelligence is recognized to be reliable. It is at some cost to ourselves that we avert our eyes from such vivid (and fleeting) clarity. If someone you described it to were to attempt to dissuade you from its authenticity, you would struggle to let it go. Who can name the source of such a recognition? In vain would we try. No need to account for it: the only *need* is to pay attention.

Sometimes in my explorations with seekers, as I'm looking for ways to guide them to see that more operates in themselves already than mere torment-generating thought, I will put this to them: "Take a few moments now to hold still, to be quiet." I let some seconds pass, then say, "Can you feel you're alive?" Here's what almost always happens: there comes another brief stretch of quiet, then their voice: "Yes." I ask how they know, how can they tell? Almost without exception what they report is that they "just know."

There are a couple of points I mean to drive home here. One is that a person is endowed with two distinct sorts of knowers. The other is this: the bodied one (unlike most of what's dished up by the one in the head) is to be trusted. To be able to tell the two apart, as life continues its unfolding, is to carry around in oneself the finest of all spiritual teachers.

In my current mode of living, both modes of intelligence are alive and well, each a blessing for the way it informs day-to-day experience. The mental one, no longer muddied up by ego-maintenance, occurs clearly and deliberately, in the thinking-about sort of way. The bodily one arrives spontaneously, out of the blue.

In the case of the latter, it's as though a great deal of "processing" has been occurring in the background, beyond conscious awareness, perhaps for a long while. I have not seen it coming. The moment of revelation may verge on startling. For what it puts before my eyes may be momentous in its ramifications for my practical life. Nor could I hope to avert my eyes from the truth just now seen. For the sudden arrival of this sort of knowing has the ring of absolute clarity. To deny it – to fail to set in motion whatever it indicates is wise or necessary – would be folly in the extreme.

Such knowing is entirely trustworthy. It's come to conscious awareness at the right moment.

This is a strange phenomenon, to be sure. For historically, a matter carrying such significance would have been either obsessively consuming of my thought patterns (generating angst and a maddening absence of clarity), or it would have been driven ferociously underground, where my frightened human self needed to keep it hidden. For the person I was then wouldn't have been able to bear the anguish of looking a discomfiting truth square in the face, when no comfortable resolution was forthcoming. Again and again I took the familiar human refuge in denial.

No more do I avert my eyes. Clarity arrives on its own schedule. When a major life change calls for processing, in my nowadays experience, it appears to have occurred in the background, without familiar mental deliberation or conscious awareness.

When one of these moments of startling knowing occurs, it's as though a committee of wise counselors, intent on my well-being, has been convening to sort out the what and the when of a major life change that's in order for me. In the rightness of time, out of the proverbial blue, I am tapped on the shoulder and handed, with palpable kindness, my marching orders.

On one occasion, it was *Time to stop leading writing workshops.* On another occasion, some years ago now, it was this: *Time for you to live alone.*

One was no greater shock than the other; I had seen neither coming. I hadn't been thinking, particularly, about either matter. Each represented enormous change in my life, and also in the lives of others. Nor did I dream of looking away from the rightness of what had been shown me. Nothing to do but grant myself the space to take in its clarity, the rightness of it, which I immediately recognized to be the case. And then to proceed with implementation, and with kindness to anyone potentially affected.

I had not, meanwhile, been engaged in the historic sort of perseverating, trying to sort out the whether-it-was-time and (if so), the when of a change. My useful mind had been blessedly unburdened, deliciously free – to marvel, reflect, discover!

One of the blessings of awakening is that it cleanses the mind of the nightmare habit of inflicting mischief on itself. As if with a surgical blade, waking up cuts out all that has been useless – the story-telling that's generated a self, devotedly defending it as if it had an objective reality – and leaves a person with a sweetly-rinsed intelligence no longer hellbent on self-inflicted pain. What's able to happen now is reflection of true benefit. Insight is able to come, and processing that yields clarity, having true value. The future can be usefully anticipated, generating not fear but potentially beneficial awareness of what may be ahead. The revisiting of the past yields neither wistfulness nor guilt, but gratitude and wisdom. Curiosity comes fully alive: you are a child again, marveling at every simple thing, as if you'd never seen it until now.

Imagine the mind – long a tormentor – now a beloved playmate, musing and whimsical. Brimming insight.

And so – in addition to the spontaneous bodily way of knowing – there is the knowledge that arrives courtesy of mental processing. These distinct knowers are alive and well in each of us, whether or not awakening has occurred. Pre-awakening, though, it's a trickier business indeed to distinguish between thinking that's ego-driven and the sort that is "clean" and of actual benefit.

Here is a clue to telling them apart: *Does having this thought bring stillness to my body, or is there uncomfortable inner "movement" just now?* Typically, such movement is circular, repetitive, one generating an emotion, and likely the resultant avoidance of that emotion. Ask yourself whether the thinking presently under way has an *egoic* means-to-an-end quality. Is its function related to self-maintenance?

The entire spiritual life, of course, can be devoted to recognizing the difference – *not conceptually* but in a real-life way – between egoic thought and the sort that's of actual benefit. One of the most common (and imprisoning) delusions about spiritual inquiry is that "knowing" the difference between these things is of any value whatsoever. The poignant irony is that this confusion is yet one more egoic application of thought: here, it is the spiritual ego supposing it's attained something of value.

My main message here, dear heart, is this: when reflecting on your mind, for God's sake do not "throw out the baby with the bathwater." To reject all-things-mental, as though the mind were entirely useless, is to miss one of the great blessings of spiritual exploration. This confusion represents one of the unfortunate misunderstandings of non-duality. Learn to sort out useless mental activity – intent on sculpting an illusory self – from magnificent (untainted!) intelligence. Notwithstanding the manifest disasters our smarts have set in motion, likely concluding in the ruination of our beloved planet and the eventual demise of our species, there's abundant evidence that *Homo sapiens* is in fact the most intelligent of mammals.

Too smart, alas, for our own good, both as a species and as individuals.

—⁓—

Sometimes I'm on the receiving end of a knowledge that seems to have come looking for me. At such a moment, there is no conceivable option but to yield, to receive.

It arrives abruptly, quietly, like a bird lighting. It's a kind of dawning, from out of nowhere: an intelligence enters my conscious awareness. Its substance is palpable, unmistakable. Something suddenly and unaccountably is *known,* with utter certainty. The foreknowing may be of something momentous. Nothing in me is inclined to doubt its authenticity, although no ordinary communication has (yet) occurred. It would not occur to me to avert my eyes.

Nor has such information been "summoned." I haven't been focusing on a particular something (wondering, speculating, anticipating). Indeed, nothing remotely on the subject has been in present-moment awareness. But here, now, something has landed. Nothing to do now but wait and see.

Soon enough.

—⁓—

*It's early morning, only barely light. I have been up awhile. It's quiet inside me as I move slowly about the house, attending to practical things. Nothing is "on my mind."*

*From out of nowhere there comes a knowing: something awful has happened in the life of a loved one, or is about to. A terrible ominous-*

*ness fills my body. I don't know who it is nor anything of the particulars. I conjecture, aware this is my mind visiting "logical" possibilities, which I do not take as reliable predictors, indicators of reality. I know only that before long I will receive external news of what-this-is.*

*Some time later – an hour, maybe two – the phone rings. It is the greatly distressed voice of my son describing having had abruptly to flee a dangerous long-term living situation, and under terrible circumstances: Covid is newly in the picture; there is no idea where to go; nor are there financial means to enable relocation. There is only the desperate need for him and his beloved partner to get out, and now.*

*Not what my mind had floated for logical possibilities (that a family member had died). Ominous, just the same. Momentous.*

*Another early morning. No one and nothing in my awareness. Then it comes, this time in the particular: my friend's heroin-addicted child is in peril, or is about to be. My heart is breaking for my beloved friend, for his precious boy. I don't know the specifics; I know only that something is under way, and that soon I will hear of it.*

*Before long, the ringing phone: the voice of my dear friend tells the nightmare of the hours before, the desperate resuscitation, the ambulance. Out of the woods . . . for now. All the stops presently being pulled out to find help for his suffering son.*

—w—

When such an episode of advance knowing occurs, nothing in me squirms to sort it out. At least, not by now: for it's happened enough times that at this point I simply nod. All that wants "doing" is the patient awaiting of what's to unfold. It's all entirely restful. I don't need to doubt the authenticity of the intelligence that's come my way. If what's ahead turns out to want my involvement, I'll see how to proceed when the time comes.

Nor are these spontaneous knowings always ominous in nature. Once, there was the clear seeing of something in my daughter's life ahead, over the unfolding years, relating to an ongoing struggle: I suddenly could *see* it would ultimately go well, become easier. Should I tell her? Would it serve her to know? I've learned to trust myself on the wisdom of such wonderings.

On another occasion, the knowledge came months ahead of the occurrence. It was to do with an upcoming election, a significant one receiving widespread attention, my own included. A good deal was riding on the outcome. Yet at the moment the foreknowing arrived, I was not at all focused on anything remotely political. My attention was altogether elsewhere just then, saturated with the immediacy of a delicious encounter with a loved one.

Suddenly, abruptly, it was here: I knew who was going to win the election. I turned my head at it. *What on earth?* It was as though the election had already occurred. But this was weeks before.

This was nothing to do with odds, nor with my own political inclinations. The certainty was so unmistakable that I thought to say something to the person I was with just then, and perhaps to one or two friends who had been fretting, fixated on one poll and another.

Should I tell them? Yet if I told anyone, I would not be able to account for the certainty. I kept it to myself. (I surely did marvel though: *You mean, I could just stop watching the polls?*)

Sure enough.

Nor (by the way) does anything in me assume I will *inevitably* receive advance notice of some significant turning point in a loved one's life. Nor in my own. I am never tempted to "go looking" – to solicit such information. Whatever source provides these moments of knowing is vastly wiser and more loving than a mere human being could hope to aspire to.

There's nothing ever to do, apart from bowing in gratitude and radical humility. In the words of T.S. Eliot,

> *The only wisdom we can hope to acquire*
> *Is the wisdom of humility.*

We are only ever on the receiving end of blessings.

—◊◊◊—

He has been the truest friend of my life – he who tended me when I supposed I was entering dementia, in the aftermath of my cat's death. By then I had grown long accustomed to his periodic "visits," having set aside my enduring skepticism.

No one in my entire life – no friend or lover, no family member – has fathomed me as he does. He knows me better than I know myself. Again and again this has been clear. Nor have I felt so altogether cherished, *unconditionally*, by anyone embodied, however beloved. His patience is boundless. I never have felt remotely judged by him.

For the first long stretch of life, my need for stability tended to win out over authenticity. I was terrified of risk. The dear one has attended me through episodes of blind repetition of old and useless patterns, through so many transitions. There were times I might be on the verge of an uncharacteristic gutsiness, contemplating taking a chance, a leap beyond what my typically tentative self would risk. I didn't always sense his presence on those occasions, until the moment had ripened into a clear resolve. It was then that I felt him. Rejoicing, laughing, as if clapping me on the back, saying *Good for you!* This happened the night I felt fear leave.

Nor when I've defaulted to my characteristic timidity has he ever judged me. Always I've felt held in radical acceptance. He's simply with me, just as I am. This is the nature of love without condition, untainted by the familiar human wish that "maybe this time she'll finally get it."

How much he has helped me to *see*.

Yet for many years I held him away, notwithstanding the seeming reality of those occasional moments when I sensed the disembodied presence of one meaning me well. I had long been reluctant to trust the authenticity of others' accounts of such experiences.

Indeed, when I would hear someone's story of a "visitor from the beyond," I'd chalk it up to the work of a vivid imagination, the expression of projected desire for such guidance. How then could I accuse myself of the same nonsense? Again and again I averted my skeptical eyes. Pretended not to feel what happened, at intervals. Struggled to dismiss, deny. Until that was no longer possible.

Again and again, at intervals, I felt *someone . . . something .
. .* in attendance. Offering guidance of a kind, some insight or encouragement. As if trying to get through to me about something. I detected a palpable tenderness, a lightheartedness. The presence seemed profoundly knowing of my interior, always to be wishing me well.

After a while, the energy it took to talk myself out of it ceased to be worth the effort, when everything in me wanted simply to engage. To take it in. To listen – if not to things exactly spoken, in a language sort of way, nevertheless unambiguous in their intent. Clearly something was being offered. It might well benefit me.

When did I at last turn frankly *toward* the presence, even unto speaking, addressing him aloud? By now this was many years ago. I recall the moment vividly, exactly where I was, when suddenly – quietly – I felt I was not alone. I was in a fast-moving car just then, apparently alone.

"Well, hello," I said aloud, as if we'd been chatty forever, as if he were sitting in the back seat. "You're here, aren't you?" I felt a smile. Always, it seems, he is prone to smile. Always wishing me well, tenderly bemused.

That night in the car, I asked to know what I might call him – how to address him. He paused a moment, then "said" (wordlessly) that if I needed to have a name for him, it could be "The One." Simply that.

A memorable experience of a visitation by a different wise and loving presence had occurred some years before I began sensing the presence of the one described above.

The encounter took place in a spacious dance studio, where I was a participant in an authentic movement class. My eyes were closed as I moved slowly about the room. In a moment of stillness, I became aware of a male presence before me. He stood close, facing. Somehow I registered that this was not one of the other embodied movers in the studio. The being was quite tall, head bowed in greeting, the palms of his hands touching, held to his chest. Appearing to know me, he seemed to be conveying palpable kindness. Gentleness.

That was all he had come to convey.

I would never forget it, nor would try. However little I was unable to account for such a thing.

—⁓—

Seekers will sometimes ask what I can tell them about the afterlife, about karma and multiple lives, the larger reality. The simple answer is nothing at all. At least, not in any way comprehensible to the ordinary mind, reducible to mere language.

Nor does it matter. Nor can I claim to "really know" any of it.

Yes, there is the sense – palpable, undeniable – of a vastness enfolding the particularity and meaning of human existence. Yet the attempt to fathom any of it lands me only in radical humility. Though I sense the relative insignificance of embodiment within the larger scheme of things, I know better than to imagine any of it could be reckoned with. At long last I've allowed myself to rest from the wish to know. (Nor will I be surprised if there does turn out to be an after.)

The real point, though, is that these things do not matter. Not now, not in this moment. For why does a person want to have some assurance, some "knowledge," of such realities beyond the immediate? We hunger for a context in which to hold the vast mystery of life, a framework for a given existence. But it's the mind wanting to know. It's the ego, accustomed to fear, aching for a scrap of control, or at least of understanding.

What use is any of it? Ask yourself: *Why does this matter to me?* In this very moment, this instant of aliveness, what can possibly matter besides being really here?

It is the most extreme – and poignant – of follies to dignify our puny minds (however curious, however "informed") by dreaming that any conceptual framework could possibly account for The Truth. It's akin to imagining we could register the endlessness of interstellar space. Best simply to bow the head in recognition of it. Let's grant ourselves permission to rest from it all. Simply to live.

We don't need an afterlife to get to paradise. Isn't that what this is all about, really?

Historically I've withheld accounts of receiving otherworldly guidance. Knowing how this terrain is woefully subject to reductive ideas and beliefs, I've been reluctant to encourage people to believe in some limiting mental notion of a larger truth. I've not wanted to contribute to belief systems, which only interfere with waking up.

Why now then do I come out with it? To bear witness to my own experience. Simply that.

Trust yourself, dear heart. Trust your own deep knowing, if it is there. Maybe that's the real message here. Just be alert to any misguided attempt to understand.

—w—

There are times when it comes to me to pray. Not in the way I prayed long ago, as a Catholic child on my earnest knees, innocently imagining I could know what to pray for, what would best serve me.

We cannot know what will serve us, or another. We only can listen. Receive.

The urge for me to pray can spring from wanting to help ease a person's torment. Perhaps it's someone who's turned to me for guidance. Yet to take the next natural step, to presume to have any sense of what to pray *for?* As if I could know what will serve a person! If I frame a prayer, it doesn't take the shape of a question or a request. The gesture expresses, simply, a receptivity – a readiness to receive whatever might be conveyed.

I grow still. The heart attunes.

Sometimes it's for myself that I indicate a receptivity for guidance. I can never know what's needed. The "only love" experience of misunderstanding what was given was a memorable lesson regarding that folly.

Nothing to do but hold still and receive. Not try too hard to understand. Then go on.

Mostly when prayer occurs, it's plain gratitude bursting my heart. *Thank you,* I cannot help but say aloud.

—␣␣—

There's one final thing I'm moved to share on the encounter with nonphysical reality.

My sweet dog Casey had been gone a few months. Though by that time she was old and greatly diminished, the timing of her death was abrupt, unforeseen. I'd imagined a different scenario for her ending, one having a more measured approach, with the space for me to be "ready." Wrong again.

With what boundless joy had Casey's youthful self celebrated the deep snow, a dolphin arcing up and down. She was fully herself in those days. Such beauty: luscious black-and-white fur, the penetrating brown eyes that saw so deeply. A friend meeting her for the first time looked up at me and softly said, *Soulful.* He'd chosen the word with great care. *That's what this dog is.* Even in her winding-down years, when she grew lame and was no longer able to see or hear so well, inside she was as she always had been.

Two enlargements of Casey's energetic young self grace my walls. Her eyes are fixed on mine. All her life it was that way: though others loved her, and she them, Casey and I belonged most truly to one another. At intervals I stand before one of the photographs, so that I may drink her in, taking solace from her having been here, with me, for a time.

In the aching days of her abrupt departure from my life, my heart was simply unable to stop breaking. It seemed the sorrow would never ease.

Now there were just two of us in the house, the aging cat Tiger and I. Casey had been Tiger's best friend. Over their many years as housemates, he had washed her doggy face, running his tongue savoringly over the long fur, around her shut eyes. So patiently did Casey allow the tender feline ministrations. They would nap together on the couch. Now, Tiger kept searching for her, visibly bewildered. Each time I entered the house, instead of greeting me, he looked past my legs to see if she would follow me in. She just kept not being there.

Where had his friend disappeared to? Tiger never got to see her dead, never got to put his nose to Casey's still body, to register her goneness in that animal way. It would have been hard to say which of us was hurting more, though I had seen her dead. I had been with her when she died. It didn't help.

Some months into Casey's absence, I was standing before one of the large photographs, looking into those brown eyes. Remembering what it was like to have her in the house, in my days. Just then, out of the blue, came a dawning. It registered in my aching heart, a thing she seemed to want me to know: that it pained her greatly to feel me hurt so hard. How startling to realize that the grief swimming in me was not solely my own.

God, I did not want to distress her! Just then, something began gently – palpably – to undo itself. Before long, the protracted sorrow was felt to ease, melting into gratitude.

There it was: Only Love.

Her stone bears the painted word *soulful.*

Years later, when it came time for Tiger to die, as I watched the vet ease the relieving needle into his arm, I whispered to Casey, *Will you greet him? He would be so happy to see you.*

And who knows? When my own time comes, perhaps the two of them will welcome me.

# The Woods as Teacher

I am constantly learning, ceaselessly incorporating into my days bits of "data" and insight, having to do with what works well and what does not. One of the primary settings of my life as a student is the woods that surround my home.

—⁓—

The northern goshawk is a ferocious creature – above all, a female during nesting season. Keeping to deep woods, the reclusive hawk is seldom seen. Local birding friends of mine have never clapped eyes on one.

It was a spring morning several years ago. Briskly moving along a familiar woods trail, I heard an unfamiliar piercing call. I stopped, moved my eyes toward its source: there she was, impressive talons curled around a branch high above my head, 50 or 60 feet from where I stood riveted. A hawk, it appeared, although one I did not recognize. Those glowering eyes were boring holes into me. I held altogether still, eyes fixed to her, memorizing her features so I could Google, back in the house, to learn what kind of hawk this was.

Had I understood the situation – what she was, why she was not merely curious about me – I would never have taken the risk of holding still. I'd have made quick feet to extricate myself from her territory, which was defined (I was soon to learn) by the presence of a recently-built nest cradling eggs from her body.

Long after, it would dawn on me that the goshawk and I were kindred, that we shared something elemental: for having given rise to young of my own, I know well the animal ferocity of a mother, when detecting threat to offspring.

Endowed with its fine mind, a human being is equipped for learning. This is equally true of a person accustomed to not living in the head. Here I am, busily making mental note of the bird's identifying features, when the much more significant learning is about to occur.

At the alarming sight of the goshawk dropping from its branch, heading with great speed toward intruder-me, my body feels the surge of adrenaline. The intelligent mammal's animal nature has now taken completely over, the mind silenced. The urgent priority is to put sufficient distance between my vulnerable body and the winged maternal fury bearing down on me.

The mind is abruptly still. But the body! Oh, it is the very opposite of the stillness that was its state only seconds before. For what's clearly under way is bodily threat (distinct from egoic "threat"). The shrieking headed for my hustling self grows louder by the heartbeat, reducing by the millisecond the distance separating my back from that open beak.

A thing about embodiment – awake or not – is this: if one's fleshly self is mortally compromised, the customary expressions of aliveness (delight, awe, cherishing) drop away. In a moment like the one I'm in, the physical assumes absolute primacy. Heart and mind activity is muted, all bodily resources rushed to the fore, courtesy of adrenaline.

I'm desperate to get the hell out of there, and quick. A remnant of background mental wisdom does fleetingly register: my sneakers mustn't move so fast as to cause me to stumble. The fleeing human animal is "re-minded," via one of its handy faculties, that tripping would enable the hellbent creature to seize the flesh-housed body now lying in the dirt, making me ever so sorry I overdid it.

Something in me has made my scurrying shoes take it down just a notch, however much my physicality insists that slowing my feet is ill-advised in the extreme. For with each rushing step, the shriek grows louder.

Closer.

—⁓—

As the Internet will later portray in ghastly detail, my mercifully intact body at rest in the computer chair, the goshawk's piercing claws and razor-sharp beak are fabulously designed to cause the clueless mammal to lament it ever presumed onto the bird's turf. I'll come upon multiple harrowing accounts of a northern goshawk making a shredded mess of a human back and scalp, when someone has been sufficiently ignorant (or foolhardy) to enter its territory.

I'll develop gigantic respect – and awe – for this creature endowed with beak and claws powerful enough to make mincemeat of even a protective helmet. The head gear had been donned by an experienced birder who "knew better" than to intrude into a nesting goshawk's territory. He was to carry lifelong scars attesting to the mistaken confidence in the hard plastic enfolding his hapless noggin. *I doubt he'll rely on that useless thing again,* I mutter into the safety of my living room.

As for me, I've learned my lesson. I'm not likely to forget what I learned that day. Another blessing of the excellent mind.

On future woods walks, I'll muse on the idea of posting a prominent sign at the turn up that trail. What it will declare is *Abandon hope all ye who enter here* (Dante's words at the gate to hell). Not that other people typically walk those trails. The sign would be for me.

As if I could ever forget.

—⁓—

For the next few springs, I went nowhere near that trail. I did miss that portion of my beloved daily odyssey among the trees – taking in the fragrant air, the sounds and colors. The distinctive features of each stretch of those woods are as dearly familiar as my own body. There are few places where I feel more alive than in that world where I'm just one of a rich variety of creatures. For the woods are *their* realm. I am a privileged guest there (if sometimes an unwelcome one).

Eventually, after a few early Junes came and went (I'd made note of the date of the encounter), I decided to venture ever so tentatively up the first rise of that trail, pausing at the turn toward the stretch where the mother bird once held court. Among the many things I'd learned about the female northern goshawk was that while she may re-use a nest over multiple years, it isn't necessarily the case.

That first time back, my feet grew still every few tentative steps, ears and eyes acutely attuned. Detecting nothing, I crept ever more cautiously toward where we met that day, stopping frequently to listen and look. At last I drew near the memorable spot, casting my eyes toward the branch where she was when we first saw one another. Nothing. I glanced in the opposite direction to the tree where I theorized the nest may have been; I'd learned about the sort of tree a nesting goshawk prefers. Seeing nothing, I proceeded slowly forward, always ready to retrace my steps.

No sign anywhere.

I have not seen her since. Perhaps she opted for a more remote part of the woods, distant from any trail, with its potential for nuisance interlopers.

As I write this, it is spring again: nesting season. As always, I will take care there to listen, to scan. When I come to that place, I will hold still. Not just from caution, but – well, to grant myself space to go back there, to the moment I met her.

For I *miss* the goshawk. How could I not? Such magnificence! How could I feel anything but great good fortune to have encountered such a creature, harrowing as the experience was?

Such ferocious maternal devotion. She and I are kindred, you see.

Until that life-altering day, I hadn't named any of the trails I walk (nor has anyone else, so far as I know). But since that pivotal experience, that stretch of my daily woods walk is the Goshawk Trail.

All my life I've loved poetry. Sometimes when I'm moving among the trees, long-beloved lines will remind me of themselves. Not long after the goshawk encounter, a famous line of Robert Frost's visited me:

*Whose woods these are I think I know.*

The speaker in the poem refers, of course, to the landowner. I had long supposed the forest surrounding my cabin to belong to my landlord, who kindly allows me to walk on his property. Now I know whose woods they really are.

I shared with the good man the news of the splendid creature who'd taken up residence in "his" woods. He was duly respectful, having long known himself to be only incidentally the *entitled* one.

Nobody owns the wild.

—⁓—

A human being under physical threat becomes primarily an animal: the focus is on survival. During the surge of adrenaline and the engagement of muscles, the processing mind takes a back seat. It does whisper helpful things like "Don't run too fast." There is evidence of the mind's usefulness, when that is needed.

The mind is also of great benefit in the department of learning, registering bits of data like *Don't come back to this trail during goshawk nesting season.* It's able to store such information, making it retrievable later.

In the time since my cat's death, something that's needed learning, and is now regularly implemented, is a comfortable moving back-and-forth between the deliciousness of pure *hereness* and the useful revisiting of context. In my life before this recent change, the transition between immediacy and the enfolding context occurred more or less automatically, as it does in most of our lives. "Context" includes not only the immediate surrounding circumstances. It also involves the mind's store of helpful information gleaned from prior experience. This periodic revisiting-of-context occurs whether I'm in the woods or out in the other sort of world, the one containing people and cars and schedules.

If in my forays into the woods I were to be *only* a body, yielding entirely to the boundless savoring of the heart, I would inevitably become lost, disoriented. My body – at this writing, soon to be 70 years old – would likely be injured, and so no longer able to spend time where I most love to be.

Were I to allow the larger truth of "what I am" to be primary, moment to moment, the expression of my *embodied* humanness would not be possible. While the experience of boundless cherishing remains the default condition, I do love being in a body! I also enjoy engaging with people, with the world we occupy together. Since the heart has assumed primacy in daily living, there's been a fresh re-discovery of other aspects of ordinary human functioning, for which I'm grateful.

Among the possible expressions of wakefulness is a balance of mammalian body experience with a richness of heart *and* efficient mental functioning. Meanwhile, with the innate capacities of a human being readily accessible, regular-life stuff is enfolded by the palpable awareness of a vastness beyond anything to do with physicality.

This is the blessing of the incarnation: we are the stuff of divinity *and* we are embodied intelligence. Even as we are mortal creatures subject to time and sorrow, something in us nevertheless knows – *feels* – that we are much more than our embodied selves.

—⚭—

*My feet are moving along a downhill trail one day in August – as it happens, the anniversary of the long-ago day awakening occurred. Since then, August 25 has felt like my truer birthday than the November date I slipped from my mother's body.*

*As I round a slight turn on the trail, something startling comes into view not many feet down from me.* My God, is that a baby bear? *Sure enough: a cub that would have emerged from its mother's body not many months ago is walking toward me, up the very trail my feet are moving down. Clearly it's unaware of me, or it wouldn't be approaching the large mammal just uphill from its little self.*

*As would be the case with any curious toddler mammal, the cub's moist nose is busily exploring the terrain just under its face. Lest the sound of my approach draw attention to my presence, I stop the movement of my sneakers. I hold altogether still, drinking in the miraculous sight.*

*Have I died and gone to heaven?* Now here's a birthday present! *I tell myself. I've seen quite a few bears out here, but never one this young – nor ever one this close up (not that I'd welcome such proximity to a grown-up). My ever-greedy self wishes time would simply stop, that this moment would last forever.*

*But the smart mammal brain animating my noggin is busily attuning to the immediate area, ears sharp, eyes moving swiftly in an ever-widening circle around me and the cub, who is meandering ever closer. For given the little one's tender age, the mama bear is surely not far away.*

*Nor would she look kindly upon my presence. Of this I am well aware. These woods I so love to explore are* her *world, not mine. I've made it my business to learn, experientially and via reading, what to do if I ever find myself in proximity to a Big Bear. Above all, a mother bear.*

*Yet as much as I know better than to linger, the heart of me simply cannot believe my good fortune: to be this near to the wee creature, who (so obliviously) continues moving its fluffy self ever closer to my legs, its nostrils snuffling up the trail's yummy scents. For in one this young and inexperienced – bear or human – curiosity tends to win out over caution. Hence the necessity of the nearby parental figure.*

*My eyes have kept up their frantic circuit, ears likewise attuned to movement in the nearby brush, or to a blood-curdling growl. Still no indication of her proximity. Nor (I can't help noticing) have I removed myself from the scene.*

Jan, if you don't put distance between you and the cub *(the data-packed head strains to remind me)*, any second now a several-hundred-pound mama will descend upon you to turn your birthday present into an unmitigated nightmare.

*Hell hath no fury like a mother's. Bear, goshawk, human: however different, deeply kindred.*

*No sign of her. By this time, the cub – still fixated on the luscious earth beneath its investigating nose – is just a couple of feet from my shoes, unaware. Within reach of my hand . . .*

*At last the maternal in me triumphs. I see I am doing the little one no favor to not "scare" it away; I'm denying it what could turn out to be a life-saving learning experience. If it continued being oblivious to the Large Mammal, a subsequent episode of proximity to a big creature, one intent upon making it into a meal (a coyote, say) may turn out to be not so benign.*

*I screw up my courage and say, softly,* Well, hello there. *The fluffy little head whips up, eyes grown comically large and round. The cub flips itself in a one-eighty. With great haste it hustles frantically through the brush up the hillside I've sometimes seen big bears travel. As though it has been bludgeoned, the baby cries out piteously for its mama.*

*Having begun my own hasty retreat, I glance toward the little one scrambling away from the scene of our encounter – toward (one can only hope) the mother, alerted to her child's desperate pleas. With no time to linger, I make quick feet in the opposite direction. Surely the mother will be more fixated on her child than on me, since by now the cub has put a fair bit of distance between us.*

*There are two blessings that day: an intact hide, and (yes) a birthday present to top them all.*

*I never do see the mother bear. Once again I've lucked out. Another piece of learning has occurred. Though this time, mercifully, the adrenaline wasn't required.*

—↝—

There is much to sort out in the aftermath of awakening. A person needs to discover a balance between the purity of consciousness and mental engagement. As the above episodes illustrate, there are times when being too much in the heartfelt now is ill-advised.

Given the profound deepening set in motion by my cat's death, with the exploded-open heart crying out for primacy, incorporating this wisdom hasn't been easy. It's asked a good deal of me; the learning is ongoing. The woods have been my great teachers in this regard. In light of how much I love spending time (life!) among the trees and my fellow creatures, the necessary expenditure has been made gladly.

Looking ahead applies to both the temporal future and the visual/spatial one. Whether anticipating something not yet here *in time* or a physical location not yet reached, seeing beyond *this* now or *this* here asks that we engage the mind and revisit its storehouse of acquired knowledge.

Sometimes, for instance, I choose (or need) to leave the familiar woods trails to step into the brush, where human feet seldom venture. The terrain there may be steep, rocky, piled with fallen branches, dense with thorns. In one way or another, this new-to-me place might be uncomfortable and possibly risky to the unaccustomed sneakers of the aging two-footed mammal. I could trip and fall, getting hurt, stepping on a woods-dweller, or damaging my shoes. The untraveled brush may well have been visited by the creatures Whose Woods These Are. There could be tucked-away nests (concealed from the eyes and noses of predators), such as a rounded cup cradling the eggs of a ground-dwelling bird. Once, most memorably, it was a buried hornet hive disturbed by my ignorant foot. It's not unusual to come upon piles of excrement deposited in the brush.

When bushwhacking, anticipating what's ahead, or could be, is valuable: *Am I headed for a pitch of terrain I won't be able safely to navigate* (and therefore might it be wise to reverse course, while that's possible)? *Is there a less thorny patch of brush I might choose than the one my foot is presently headed for?* My bushwhacking-savvy daughter has helped me do better at looking ahead when we're in the woods, because that is what she routinely does. She has, with evident bemusement, watched her oh-so-present mother head witlessly into a thorny tangle, when I might have spotted (if only I'd glanced ahead) a nearby alternative route containing no thorns whatever. I've learned a good deal from my capable and patient daughter.

All of which has been grist for the mill, information to tuck away for future bushwhacking adventures. The mind is a handy device to consult in such situations. Its storehouse is ever-growing, so long as I keep eyes and ears attuned in my adventures off the trail.

In the same vein, I have learned (the hard way) that if I should trip while briskly moving along with my cold hands tucked in my pockets, the likelihood of being able to catch myself on my extended palms isn't as good as it would have been with arms at my sides. It takes a millisecond to get the hands from the pockets, which is about how long it takes to do a face-plant in the dirt. The moral of the story: if it's a chilly day, gloves are in order.

I make it my business to pay attention to the timing of various hunting seasons in Vermont, so that when those days arrive, I do one of two things: walk instead on the dirt road, or (knowing as I do that few hunters venture into the woods where I walk) I wear a bright orange vest meant to proclaim my presence to the eyes of anybody within shooting distance. I also clap my hands or blow a whistle at intervals.

Here is a much-appreciated feature of the background learning that accompanies me everywhere: it's all carried *quietly* in the back of my head, readily retrievable when circumstance calls for it. This is conspicuously different from what happened with kindred learning in my prior life. In the old me, my brain would've been obsessively re-minding me of the what-to-do-ifs. This made for a ceaseless (and noisy) loop. Is it any wonder, then, that I was seldom fully *there?* Anxiety, in those days, was a constant companion. Cautionary wisdom wasn't able to live tucked quietly in the back of my head. Nowadays it handily dwells there, curled up and snoozing like a contented dog, ready to spring into action at a moment's notice.

My numerous observations of bears in the woods have taught my ears to recognize telltale movement in the nearby brush. Nor would I think to pay undue regard to any sign of proximity. I understand the need, on detection, to hold still. If the bear sees me, so long as a respectable distance separates us, I know to allow the much larger mammal to be the one to make the first move – which will, almost certainly, be *away* from me. I also carry a handy background knowledge of what I'd need to do in the event of inadvertent close proximity to a bear. I've educated myself (thank you, Google) as to the prudent posture and movement to adopt in such a situation. I learned that a bear ticks somewhat like a domestic dog, which tends to read turning-and-fleeing as an invitation to give chase. While everything in a person might naturally have the instinct to run, doing this with a bear (which can easily outrun one of us) would be a very bad idea. The thing, then, is *slowly* to back away, maintaining eye contact, all the while attempting to appear as large as possible. This is crucial particularly if the bear has risen to upright on its hind feet, the posture of aggression. If I were wearing a backpack at the time, I would reach behind to the underside of the pack, still facing forward, and attempt to raise it above my head. Failing that, simply extending my arms above my head would suffice.

Fortunately there hasn't been the need to implement this guidance about close proximity. Generally, when a bear and I have clapped eyes on one another, we've simply held still, scrutinizing each other from a distance. Then, when it felt ready, the bear has moved off into the brush, enabling me to proceed down the trail. This happened on one of my trail walks, part of which involves retracing steps taken several minutes prior. I had just rounded the sharp turn back to home, giving me a long view of the trail ahead, when I saw a bear cross the trail several hundred feet away. It saw me just when I saw it. Both of us grew still, checking out one another. Given the significant distance separating us, I felt no concern whatever, this not being bear cub season.

Something I've learned online is how to distinguish an adult from an adolescent. If I squat to come near the ground, and there's daylight between the furry belly and the patch of earth it stands on, it's more likely young than full-grown. The belly of an adult tends to come near the ground, when it's on all fours. But when a bear is pretty far away, as this one was, it can be challenging to get a reliable "read" on the creature's size. I guessed this one to be an adult.

After a timeless minute or so – I was transfixed – my fellow looker seemed to lose interest, and ambled on across the trail, headed downhill into the brush. I proceeded, then, to walk on. As I approached the place the bear had stood not long before, I paused and listened. I gazed in the direction I'd seen it go, my own feet where its had just been. Was there any sign, any sound? Nothing discernible. The mighty creature had melted into the brush, gone on to other adventures.

It dawned on me, at some point, that the moment of our mutual sighting probably had constituted the bear's *second* view of me: for only a handful of minutes before, I had walked past that very place. A bear's ears and nose are exquisitely attuned in a way our own are woefully inept. Doubtless it had heard or smelled my approach, silently pausing for me to go by. Having then detected my goneness (just about the time of my habitual turnabout, retracing my steps), the bear resumed its travel – toward, as it happened, my own intended route.

I'll wager the bear retained no memory of the sighting. As for me, though this occurred years ago, I have never forgotten the moment. Seldom do I round that turn that my recollecting heart doesn't *see* that bear down there, seeing me. What a privilege it was.

Reminding me that among the trees, we are seen and sniffed ten thousand more times than we know.

—⚬—

In spring, summer, and fall, my woods walks take place almost entirely on the familiar trails. The defined paths generally travelled by my sneakered feet are easiest on my body. The hilly terrain the trails move over offers plenty of up-and-down to keep muscles healthy, including the crucial one in the aging chest. There are fewer fallen twigs to trip over; most stones are well anchored, making them readily traversable. The occasional indentations in the earth, ready to collect falling rain and thus prone to turn muddy and slippery, are familiar features I know to watch out for.

I do need to attune to the possible presence of others on the bit of earth my heavy foot is about to descend upon: one of the first tiny bluets of the season, its delicate pale petals just now unfolded; perhaps a meandering slug, or an early-spring garter snake come to luxuriate in a patch of warming sunlight. The brilliant orange newt just ahead of my hurrying sneaker, the chipmunk hurtling across where my foot is just this second about to land. Some creatures, less welcome, tend to keep to the dense brush left and right of the trail. Lyme-bearing ticks, for instance, are less likely to set up housekeeping on a cleared trail regularly tamped down by heavy human feet.

In non-winter seasons, the familiar network of defined trails is the way to go. But in winter! Oh, the entirety of the rapturous forest becomes blessedly accessible, even to the feet of an elder. Deep snow – especially with snowshoes fastened to my boots – makes readily available even daunting hills and deep ravines with steeply-pitched sides, altogether forbidding in another season. In winter, woods plants have fewer leaves. Even boulders, substantial downed tree limbs, and tangles of thorny branches are rendered navigable when enough snow has fallen to bury them. It's all tucked away beneath the sweet white blanket that makes everything look . . . well, very much like everything else. Snow has a wondrously equalizing quality about it. The winter forest is not its familiar-looking self, bisected by trails I know almost like I know my own body.

In addition to the beneficial glancing ahead at unfamiliar terrain during bushwhacking, there is also the looking ahead that's temporal rather than spatial in nature. If I'm heading out for a snowy woods exploration, perhaps it would be wise to venture out earlier than mid-afternoon. The brain might handily re-mind me that winter days are short. And that it's likely to be colder once night has fallen. Spontaneity is generally delicious, but it is not always smart.

While I need to take care, in non-snow seasons, not to venture too far from the familiar path, lest I become disoriented and lost, it's another matter altogether in winter. Snowshoes are wondrous devices, making it possible to traverse terrain unwelcoming in non-snow seasons. I can explore to my heart's content, assured that the trail laid by the biting impressions of my meandering snowshoes will be retraceable, followable all the way home, when I decide to turn and head back. It means I need pay no attention at all to where I've made random turns, dictated by the moment's whim.

But on one occasion – most memorably – I became profoundly disoriented in the snow-blanketed woods. This time, atypically, I had ventured out in the middle of a heavy snowstorm, the fast-falling snow having erased the path marked by my toothy snowshoes. Although while the ongoing erasure was under way, so focused was I on the immediate delight of where I was and what I was seeing and feeling, I was unaware of what was steadily taking place right behind me. (Perhaps there is not so much difference between a curious bear cub and an allegedly intelligent human being.) Meanwhile, having no sense of the gathering risk, I was continuing obliviously into territory altogether unfamiliar to me, with no idea how far from home I was, nor what direction my house might be in.

Once there's plenty of snow on the ground, even on a sunny day, it can be challenging to recognize even the most familiar defined walking trails. Snow obliterates trails that are otherwise readily apparent. Never mind how "familiar" the terrain. Because the trees are mostly bare of their greenery, the spaces between them are more substantial in winter than in the growing seasons, when a more readily visible broad "line" is drawn among the trees by the spacious winding trail, on which nothing much grows. But in snow-covered woods, when the leaves are down, the familiar pathways through the woods are not so obviously detectable. The white stuff is a remarkable equalizer.

It's surprisingly easy to become disoriented. Lost.

This oh-so-memorable occasion happened late enough in that winter afternoon, with dark fast approaching, that I could well have been stranded overnight in the forbidding conditions. Nor was the lowering sun of any help in the matter of determining direction, concealed as it was by the curtain of heavy falling snow.

There is no cell service out there.

Mercifully I managed to find my way to the welcome sight of my landlord's cleared field coming into view. By chance I'd come upon a familiar tree, one I knew well from the foot trail. It resembles no other tree in those woods, thanks to a defining feature of its bark-stripped trunk: an encircling impression left by the teeth of a long-ago chain saw. When that tree came into view, I grew very still. My humorous backward-looking self pictures enfolding angelic light transforming the signpost into a "vision" (like a cheesy moment in a movie). I can laugh now, but that is precisely how that sighting landed in me. I used the tree as a way to orient myself. In short order I was able to get my bearings. Courtesy of that tree – I wanted to wrap my arms around it and kiss it – I was able to detect the shape of the snow-blanketed trail I've traveled ten thousand times, to see which way I must now turn and proceed, to find my way out of the woods before dark.

A good deal of learning surely did occur that day.

—⁂—

People longing to wake up sometimes hold mistaken impressions about what radical freedom is like. Some suppose that the quieting of the mischief-causing mind, long in the thrall of ego-maintenance, leaves a person in a kind of clueless la-la land. This is far off the mark. What actually happens, for most, is that the mind simply no longer inflicts suffering. Instead, it's blessedly freed up to be of actual use. It can learn; it can remember. The liberated mind becomes a *practical* device, a handy tool to be implemented when a life situation warrants its engagement.

If I hadn't had a working mind that day I got lost in the stormy woods, things may not have turned out so well. But here's the real miracle: not once did I feel fear, even as I was looking square in the face of the reality that I may indeed not find my way home before dark. There was no mental space to spare – to squander! – on being afraid. There was no furious mother goshawk to escape; adrenaline was not needed. What was in order was for me to think: to see if I could sort out, in a logical way, where I was, what direction to go.

Yes, the marked tree surely helped me get my bearings. But I was also aware of needing to travel in a general downhill direction, not to get to my house, but to find my way to the residence of my landlord, who has a maple sugaring operation. Parts of the woods I travel are made up of maple trees, many of which are tapped. A vast network of sap lines grids those patches of maples. The sugar house (where the sap will be boiled down, in spring, to syrup) is downhill from most of the lines, gravity enabling the sap to flow to its destination.

The sugar house is on my landlord's property, in a clearing beside the road, and from there, I knew I could find my way to my own home. Which indeed I did, just before night fell.

Fear ran my life for 50 years. Once upon a time, after such an experience, the story of that snowy afternoon would have become a "thing" in my head, an endlessly repeating nightmare shimmering with anxiety. I'd have carried it like a burden I could not put down, along with the countless other difficult experiences I never got over. Instead, the lessons I learned that day – what to do, what not to do – rest quietly tucked away in the back of my head, retrievable at a moment's notice, should they ever be needed. Thus is the gift of a liberated mind, one no longer devoted to suffering.

# Discoveries, Explorations, and Surprises Galore

## Heart, Mind, and Body

In the 20 years since awakening, I've observed several chapters in the fuller waking-up of my heart, mind, and body. Prior to 2003 my primary experience of life occurred via the heart, with the oh-so-busy mind never ceasing its tormenting commentary. I had always been very much in my body (if also identified with its features). While it was the suffering heart that appeared to catalyze the initial moment of awakening, in the long stretch of life to unfold afterward, the focus – to my frank surprise – was on the blossoming mind.

In retrospect, that's not so odd. For although I'd always had a "good" mind, as the world sees such things (I'd been an accomplished student, a skilled writer), the greater portion of my mental life had been devoted to the upkeep of the illusory self. The forging of identity, the obsession with past and future, fretting and grasping for control – these were the occupations of my intelligence. Which is to say, it was squandered almost entirely on fruitless and pain-generating undertakings.

Imagine the breath of fresh air, then, when so much space was abruptly freed up in my noggin. The departure of fear and attachment, and the fading of my lifelong fixation on identity, endowed me with the miracle of limitless space for contemplation, curiosity, awe, and the ever-human attempt to fathom. *None of it generating angst.* To my heart's content I explored terrain newly of compelling interest: like the question *Why doesn't everybody experience life* this *way?* (Why indeed hadn't I, my first five decades?) Then came the dawning of this idea: *Given that it's now so obvious that this radical peace is actually everybody's innate condition, might there be something I could do to . . . help them* see? Could I show others the way to freedom from mind-generated suffering – to get that it's not, in fact, inevitable?

During the period of my mind's blossoming, the lifelong heart tenderness was still in evidence. I also continued to enjoy being embodied, although the familiar *identification* with physicality (and the associated fear) had melted away.

As life carried on, bit by bit there was growing attention to my body. This was in part because of having learned the wisdom of looking ahead, both visually (as in the woods) and temporally. I began registering that I didn't have forever to live. With the growing focus on physicality, I felt my body come more entirely alive. I took better care of it, eating a healthier diet and getting regular exercise. *Not* to "avoid death" (ha!) but simply to enjoy being here, for however long that may last.

Then my beloved cat died, setting in motion all that unfolded from there . . . landing me back, now absent crippling fear, in the dominant terrain of life pre-awakening: the heart. And so – perhaps ironically (since it was where I'd started) – the heart was to be the final realm where the full blessing of awakening would be experienced.

In the years since my cat's death, having learned how to re-engage with the physical and mental realities of a human life, the mind has come once again to do a good deal of learning – some of it to do with reveling in the physical life.

—∭—

## *Orientation to Time and Mortality*

For many years after I woke up, I was altogether content being in the present moment. Seldom did I look ahead over the long term, the matter of what might lie ahead. I'd been miraculously relieved of the future-focused terror I'd been run by all my life, which hadn't been so much about the dread of death as it was about the fear of running out of time to finally get things "right." Never could I hold still, back then: doing so would have constituted (most ironically) wasting time.

When the machinery of fear unwound, the ferocious attachment to goal-achieving melted into the sweet now. When the goals disappeared, they took with them all the meaning fastened onto them: that could I somehow fulfill them, that would mean *I'm a good mother, so my life is worthwhile.* Departing fear took with it the familiar understanding of meaning and attachment. It also meant – talk about blessing! – that I could finally truly rest. Relaxing no longer needed to be "earned," as it had my whole life prior, with anxiety and the drive to *do* fueling ceaseless activity.

Before awakening, I'd wanted life to go on and on, so I'd have time to achieve what I believed would fulfill me. Also, of course, I wanted to postpone death, the radical cessation of all possibility. I used to tell myself that once I got done with all that needed doing, *then* I could rest. I was haunted by the dwindling of time, the hourglass holding fewer grains than the day before. The timing of my demise – the number of days remaining – was agonizingly unknowable. No wonder I had a paralyzing breakdown in my thirties.

I postponed delight for the sake of what "needed" doing. The sense of priority regarding the spending-of-time was radically out of whack. Death was the enemy. What I feared was running out of time, the most precious of all commodities. The irony of it! For the now is time-*less*-ness.

But guess what? The list of what needs doing, for all of us, is endless. Then we die. Both are true: we don't have forever to be in the stillness of the now.

Now my days were one vast welcome sigh of relief. It was purely delicious to be able fully to rest: to enjoy being here, for its own sake. No longer was life about doing (or failing-to-do). It was about being, and reveling in plain being. Existence simplified to the point where the only needs were the physical ones, the animal requirements for water, food, and protection from the elements. Emotional need was gone.

I had stopped focusing on the passage of time. Given that I was no longer driven by fear and need, or attachment to getting what I desired, the experience of *preferring* didn't enter the picture of post-awakening life for some years. Given that acceptance had become the norm, the business of wanting, for the most part, wasn't on the landscape of my days.

Before awakening, any sense of preference had been fastened onto needing-to-have. Now, given that I was ceaselessly content, it simply didn't dawn on me that I might nevertheless really *want* to do one thing or another with whatever remained of this life.

In the stillness of freedom after I woke up, acutely aware of how much pain people were in, I was entirely content to allow loved ones' desires, as well as the wishes of those seeking my guidance, to determine how I lived. I deeply understood that it took nothing from me to do so. Primarily I was responsive, my own potential preferences seldom occupying space in awareness. During this era, I seldom considered the truth that one of these days life would inevitably come to an end.

Waking up had caused mortality to stop feeling like an enemy. Imagine my surprise, after years of immersion in the now, with no sense of the larger temporal context, when I began to notice myself weirdly paying more attention to how I spent my days. The notion of having priorities began to enter awareness. Bit by bit it started dawning on me that I didn't have forever to do a given thing I might enjoy, or might really want to do.

It came to pass that brevity began gently to remind me of itself. I sat up and took notice. This was new! The revelation occurred when I was in my late fifties, about ten years into awakening. I reflected on the diminishment that could come with advancing age: *Given that I will one day die, might there be some things I'd like to do while I'm still able?* Not merely alive, but fit enough to be active, to have the energy for (say) a travel adventure with my son.

I did not have forever! What opened up was a blossoming sense of opportunity on the landscape of what might be ahead. And – most surprising and life-altering – was this: I began to have real preferences as to how I lived. Such a welcome (and delicious!) revelation: that just because I no longer resisted or feared anything didn't mean I might not have preferred modes of being.

To experience the newfound freedom to realize I had option, and to have the palpable delight of implementing desired changes in my practical life, was one of the long-term blessings of fear's departure. As I usefully considered what might lie ahead for my aging self – even as I couldn't know how long I had left, nor what would befall me – I began to register how much I love being alive.

Since awakening, I'd paid little attention to the well-being of my physical self. I now see this was natural, in light of how prior body attention had been fear-driven. Now came a brand new orientation to my body – not to avoid death, not because of the life-long identification with the body, but simply to enable my aging self to drink in the luscious world and its waiting adventures. I found myself hoping I had decades of living ahead. This continues to be the case, notwithstanding the manifold disasters of our aching world.

What a surprise: to find myself inspired to notice my aging body, tenderly caring for it, the way I would look out for my cat's well-being, as I once tended my babies. So strange – and delightful – to be moved to care for my physical self, *rinsed of the lifelong identification with it.* A breath of fresh air!

The motivation to care for myself was simply that I loved life. Living was fun! Why wouldn't I want to enable myself to have more experiences with those dear to me? To spend leisurely time in the woods and do other things I enjoyed? The altered orientation to my body occurred without attachment to outcome, with no illusion of control or predictability.

I had long known I was susceptible to diabetes, both from being overweight and from genetic tendencies. I knew if I were to get the disease, I'd adjust as necessary. Meanwhile, I figured daily life would be less complicated if I didn't have to take insulin. I changed my eating habits and began taking daily walks in the woods.

Since there's no knowing how much time remains, what a person most longs to do mustn't be put off. Meanwhile, my much older body is in better shape than it's been in decades. I used to have to pay a neighbor to stack my cord wood, in summer, for keeping warm in winter. Now I revel in stacking it myself. I take good care of my physical self, even as I'm aware of the inevitable diminishing aging brings.

Orienting this way to my brevity has been a revelation. The world of delight opened up even beyond what it had been before. How did I most want to spend my days? How might my newly-acknowledged preferences shape the way I lived?

My orientation to time had shifted. I now saw an actual benefit to looking ahead. This development signaled a huge turning point in my post-awakening life. Such fun: to ask myself what I would *like.* To grant myself the space to take into account my own wishes, perhaps giving them priority over someone else's (even as I knew the change might disappoint or bewilder them).

A kind of bucket list began forming. How quickly then was the celebratory trip with my now-sober son set in motion. At that time he was newly out from under the ravages of heroin addiction. I asked if he'd like to see the redwoods. He lit up like a little boy.

In short order we had airline reservations for a celebratory odyssey to northern California. Those luscious days of togetherness, with nothing to do but talk deeply (our conversations having never resorted to the superficial), to gaze at the extraordinary woods giants, to meander across the Golden Gate Bridge and along broad Pacific beaches, remain among the highlights of both our lives.

Then it was one thing after another in my life, having to do with the everyday and also relating to more adventures of the sort my son and I had enjoyed. Here was the real surprise: this dramatic inner change significantly altered how my ordinary days were spent, changing long-familiar modes of living. In addition to the question of how I might most like to spend whatever time remained, there came a blossoming preference for solitude. And for simplicity in all things, which resulted in a growing focus on efficiency and on economizing, of both effort and material resources. I loved taking my time with all things, having the space for savoring, wishing never to have to rush. I delighted in having as little to do as possible in a given stretch of time, enabling a luscious spontaneity. The less I had scheduled, the better I liked it. There grew a clear desire to minimize, as much as possible, the need for mental engagement. Much revision of a long-familiar way of living was set in motion.

What had come alive in me, after so many years of radical equanimity with whatever-it-was, was the enlivening energy of preference. The feel of wanting to do this rather than that. To live this way, not so much that. There came one revelation after another of the ways preference seemed to want to express itself in how I lived.

Notably, each expression of desire was blessedly rinsed of the long-familiar attachment to getting the wanted thing. If something I desired didn't materialize, or if it did come about but then didn't last (nothing does!), I was entirely fine with those developments. No clinging anywhere. A breathtaking discovery, such wondrous freedom in it. It simply had never dawned on me, all the years since awakening, that I could *want* without being desperate to *have*. In our ordinary human way of being, the two come hand-in-hand: yet it's not inevitable that it be so!

How my life did revolutionize itself, in short order. The things I did, the ways I lived, how my days were spent. There were many surprising developments along the way, things I'd not seen coming. One long-familiar pattern after another simply undid itself, leading me in a brand new direction. Along the way, much more unstructured space was brought about in my days.

Having no idea how long I had left, I set about making plans to realize the few items on my bucket list. For many years I had dreamed of seeing and hearing Randy Newman perform his music. Not long after the revelation about brevity, I found myself sitting front-and-center in a theater in Boston, where the gifted songwriter sat at his piano and regaled a gathering of his most devout fans. That evening was one of the musical high points of my life. It was a birthday gift to myself: the concert happened to fall on the anniversary of the November date my body left my mother's.

When waking up happens, desire and hope do not cease to live in a person. It's just that we no longer *have* to get what we might want. Nothing is any longer riding on some possible future. As I was joyfully anticipating that night with Newman and his music, I was well aware that if my car were to break down en route and I never actually got to the concert hall, I would be entirely fine. Considering with what keen pleasure I anticipated being in that theater with the beloved musician, such non-attachment is something of a miracle.

This past summer, my daughter and I boarded a train and headed west, then south, our destination the Grand Canyon. How can it be that the trip there and back in the cozy roomette, the rocking back and forth across a good part of this huge country, which we watched out our window – that the getting there, and then home again, turned out to be every bit as memorable as the vast canyon itself? If surely of a different order of reality: I know better than to attempt to describe what it was to stand in its unfathomable presence.

Nor will its vast silence ever leave me, although my body is no longer there beside it.

—ⱳ—

## *Being Kind to Myself: The Cost of a Thing*

A guiding light in my nowadays life is the wish to be kind to myself. As I've carried on, there's been a blossoming awareness of the cost of exertion – of pushing myself, physically or otherwise. I've come to be gentler on my aging self, and it feels delicious.

Though I didn't initially see this through the lens of kindness-to-self, I'd come to detect a subtle effort involved when engaging with others. By then the preference to linger in the spaciousness of the heart had come to predominate. The default mode was to sense whatever was in the field of awareness as a subtle continuity. In felt oneness, familiar boundaries are much softer than how a person typically experiences them. The effort I sometimes felt in social encounters appeared related to the need to adopt the "pretense" of a distance separating myself from the other person. In order to have a conversation, it's necessary to experience a *you* and a *me*.

Attuning to this dynamic occurred quite a few years ago by now. It would ultimately lead to the preference to live alone, to be mostly in solitude. This continues to be the case even as (yes!) I love being with people dear to me. It's well worth the "cost" of the effort, enabling me to engage Like a Regular Person.

Recently, being kind to myself has found other expressions, including declining to hurry or to multitask. Here is the guiding question nowadays: "Is this worth it?" Each thing we do, whether or not we're aware of it, asks something of us: energy, time, and perhaps forgoing something else. To attune to this sort of cost, to be real with oneself, is to orient to life and limited energy with tender regard. Everything has a cost, the money sort of expenditure being the very least of it.

*Is it worth it?* Increasingly the answer is no. Pausing to put this question to myself has become a kindly prodder, a reminder to take into account the larger picture of what something under consideration will likely entail. It's the business of any action carrying inevitable consequences, one thing leading to another. I ask myself the question, for instance, when contemplating anything new.

If the answer is *Yes indeed!*, with what sweet gladness do I proceed. Playing, as ever, with a full deck. The more precious life comes to be, the more we owe it to ourselves to be real about what we take on. For something to be "worth it," it's essential that I look square in the face the matter of what the contemplated item will ask of me. I take care not to ignore any quiet whispering that I-might-wish-I-hadn't-done-this. Then again, most anything can be let go in a heartbeat. So . . . is it worth giving this a shot? Maybe I put it that way to myself. It's a way of being loving to myself.

In my own case, cost has also to do with whether a thing will require mental engagement (crucial, since I prefer not thinking), as well as the prospect of its needing me to drop some other wanted (or necessary) item. Given that my favorite mode is ease, with a minimal structure to most of my days, that's where any consideration of introducing something new inevitably begins. My underlying priority is to have as little as possible on my to-do list. Spontaneity is delicious.

Once upon a time, I prided myself on the ability to multitask. Other people, observing the "skill," admired me for it. As if it were good to be able to do two things at the same time. In my own inner observations, I came to realize that even attempting to think while engaging in a physical task constitutes multitasking. In that case, we are struggling to bring attention, simultaneously, to what's inside the head *and* to what the body's doing.

I once heard a brain scientist describe the chemistry of what occurs inside the head during an attempt to multitask. How in fact what's happening, with lightning speed, is a darting back-and-forth, back-and-forth, between focus on the two items. That is, we are *not*, in fact, doing two things simultaneously. He explained how doing so is in fact taxing to the brain – tiring to the very person who imagines that it "has" to be this way, with "so much to get done." His portrayal brought to vivid life how attempting to do two things at once means neither is done as well as it might have been, had we granted ourselves permission to do one thing, then the other. Hence – ironically – time might actually be *saved:* for to do something once, with full attention, likely means it won't have to be redone later.

The poor scrambling brain, all the while, is furiously attempting to focus in two directions at once. The result (surely you have observed this) is that after you go out to do errands, it dawns on you that you're not certain you turned off the stove as you'd intended to. Why does this happen? It's because you – because we, for I noticed myself in this same wasteful process – simply cannot attend two things at once. One of them, or more likely both, ends up being less well done for lack of sufficient attention.

By the time of this writing, it's been years since all of this became clear in my awareness. I long since learned that if I try to think while turning off the stove, I'll have to go back later to be certain it's turned off. Or I will need to revisit whatever thought I'd been having while my hand was turning the knob. Nowadays, on the unusual occasion when I try to do two things at once, I stop myself and say: *Which matters more in this moment?* Shall I think first and then do the task, or is it better to hold still and contemplate, and *then* do the physical thing?

When thinking occurs *consciously* – that is, when it happens deliberately, not (as it long was) unconsciously, often saturated in emotion – then it's entirely possible to set thought aside for the duration of an action requiring full attention. If something is worth doing, whether it's mental or physical, it merits the fullness of conscious awareness.

Spending so much time in the woods has provided me unending opportunities for learning along these lines. This includes discovering how attempting to think while moving is unwise, sometimes even dangerous. How many times have I tripped over a fallen twig, because of focusing on the exciting new thing that just now dawned on me, to the detriment of attuning to my ever-aging feet? Walking briskly through trees full of enthralling creatures, most of whom are heard more than seen, is a real set-up for losing my footing. It is crucial for my well-being that my ears and eyes be attuned to the possible proximity (for instance) of an irritated mother bear during the time of young cubs. Much of what my senses drink in is not of the nature of safety, but of pure delight: the glorious song of the veery in the treetops to my left; the magnificent sight of the soaring pileated woodpecker with its gaudy red head. But fully to take in these moments among the beloved trees, I must hold still. Not just so I don't stumble, but so as not to divide attention in a way that sacrifices one scrap of the moment's savoring.

It's like the thing my musician brother once said to me: if you "listen" to music as a kind of background to daily activities, you aren't really – fully – *listening*. How right he was. Nowadays if I've got music playing, it's front and center in awareness. The moment I notice myself pulled to do something else, I turn it off. Music I love is worth every drop of attention.

Once a person (awake or otherwise) realizes – in a bodied way, not in the head – that there is latitude over where attention is put in a given moment of consciousness, much becomes possible. We can be deliberate about where attention is placed. Here is another expression of being kind to myself. Once or perhaps twice a day, I consciously "attend" matters to do with the larger world. This includes the sorts of concerns showing up on the news: the current situation with the Covid pandemic, ongoing wars (like the one in Ukraine), the state of American democracy, of the climate crisis. There is much to do with the random slaughter of children, of people of color.

These things matter to me, as they do to most of us. But I don't "live" there all day, even as I'm well aware the phenomena are ongoing. I know how much tuning-in to these realities is enough and how much is unnecessary, in order for me to stay sufficiently in touch with what goes on around me, across the world. Much about our planet is a mess. It is heartbreaking. Yet it's not difficult to be deliberate in the matter of how much attention to bring to a given concern. As a result, although my heart will surely break in the presence of the many nightmare conditions in our world, I do not linger there unnecessarily.

During the time my son was actively using heroin, aware as I was that he could die at any moment, I nevertheless did not dwell, hour after hour, in awareness of the tentative state of his aliveness. I simply loved him with my wide-open heart. In no way did I wall off the love, in the name of "protection." Of course I knew how his dying, should it occur, would crush me. There's no contradiction between the two.

Nor does the awareness of the severity of such things interfere with the deep peace that carries me along. This does not constitute denial. Such things would've been hard to understand, prior to awakening, when any painful or challenging reality tended to take fierce hold of me and keep me in its grip. Something said, "If it's real in an ongoing way, then I must be tuned into it in an ongoing way." That is, obsessed.

No wonder I suffered. No wonder we human beings suffer.

Please consider this possibility for yourself. It is not necessary to awaken in order for you to learn about the latitude regarding your attention, in any moment you become self-aware. Do note: attention is not the same as thinking-about. It's got to do, simply, with where you put your inner eyes. Where your momentary focus is.

Consider the expression *pay attention:* it's right there, in the way we say that. Attention is a commodity, and it is a most precious one. More precious by far than the money sort of commodity.

—⁓—

It's been my way, for some years now, to economize wherever possible. This is to conserve resources, to minimize my adverse impact on the environment. The incentive to economize has also to do with minimizing the need to generate income. Given that my preference is for mostly unscheduled days, it follows that income-generating work be kept to a reasonable level. For a modest income to be feasible, I need to take care to hold down the cost of utilities. I use only whatever lights are necessary, always taking care to turn them off when not needed.

This past winter was my new cat's first cold season with me. Her love of the toasty wood stove collaborated with my econo-mizing to create the occasion for a memorable lesson. The learn-ing took place at some cost to me, and very nearly to my cat. On this particular morning, the stove was cranked up to quite hot, the world out the windows being mighty chilly. My children were about to visit for the day, and I wanted the house to be warm and welcoming. The hotter-than-usual stove was a magnet to my fellow mammal, who loves nothing more than heat. Golde had her oh-so-golden self tucked almost beneath the iron box, in a rapture of toastiness, when the allegedly intelligent mammal walked in front of the stove, en route to someplace. In the name of holding down costs, the living room was dimly illumined just then, so I didn't see her.

Mercifully, as my slippered foot began its downward pressure *smack dab onto that furry body,* which it would break my heart to in-jure or even to frighten, my flattened fleshy palm swiftly responded by landing square on the top of the oh-so-hot stove. This enabled me to achieve two important things: not step on Golde and also not trip, potentially injuring myself in the fall onto the hard floor, against the wall of the stove.

The cat, of course, was startled, although – ever her feline self – was shortly restored to her prior cozy state beside the raging box of heat, her accustomed equanimity likewise restored. Meanwhile, the "intelligent" upright mammal was swiftly able to access prior learn-ing about the urgency of treatment in the case of a severe burn. I began implementing, with all due speed, the necessary steps to minimize the damage to the now-cooking hand flesh. The goal was to aim for something short of a third-degree burn. I was well aware I had (gladly) just subjected myself to the prospect of considerable damage to my palm, which I realized was about to be out of service for some time. This, on my dominant right side.

The priority, for the first stretch of awareness, was to attend the body – even as I was surely aware, in a background sort of way, that a bit of learning had already been set in motion. First was the plunging of the sizzling hand beneath the rushing cold faucet. Then the generous application of cold aloe gel (kept in the refrigerator for such occasions), followed quickly by the swaddling of the hand, a small ice pack tucked inside the containing cloth. Aware my daughter was in possession of a supply of gauze, I phoned her, hoping she hadn't yet left home to head north to my house, and alerted her to what had happened. I asked her to come bearing whatever she had that might be of use. I was also aware that her training to become a physician would hold her (and her idiot mother) in good stead, as she'd recently learned about the degrees of skin burns, the layers of epidermis, et al. Before long, she arrived armed and ready.

The pain in my hand was considerable, for some hours. My grown-up children were able to assume some of the roles that their maternal host had supposed she'd be playing, in the delivery of the meal I'd prepared for us all. We had, as ever, a fine time together, notwithstanding the hand-burning drama preceding their arrival. Among the delights had by the young people was spending time with Golde, she who'd occasioned the unfortunate event. By the time we all embraced goodbye, some hours later, the pain in my hand had begun somewhat to ease. I anticipated keeping it swaddled for a few days, relying primarily on my left hand.

Miraculously, by the next morning, I found myself unswaddling the damaged goods, to take a peek at how the skin was doing. While the palm was quite red, and certainly tender, to my surprise only one small portion of flesh had blistered. The pain, by then, had pretty much disappeared, so long as I took care not to use the hand. It turned out my speedy burn-prevention measures had paid off. I replaced the bandage my daughter had applied, relying mostly, over the coming days, on my left hand. In the end, very little skin was to peel.

Meanwhile, a brightly-illumined lesson had formed itself in conscious awareness: *It's worth only so much to save on electricity.* Lesson learned: when in doubt, leave the light on.

What a blessing I'm endowed with fast reflexes: for not only had I been able to move with due speed to lift my stepping foot, but also I managed simultaneously to plant my balancing hand on the stove. I thereby prevented a fall onto my cat . . . right beside the hard-and-hot stove, where I'd doubtless have injured myself yet worse than the damage inflicted to my hand. Reflexes do not involve thinking: they occur much more swiftly (even in this old-lady body) than the sluggish mind operates.

A beneficial limberness is another quality of my physicality – and, as it happens, of my mind. The mental limberness shows up in the absence of attachment to habit. The person I used to be was fiercely attached to any habit I found useful in daily living. The attachment was driven by fear and the desire to control. I was loathe to let go any regimen that had proven reliable. Such rigidity is no friend to us. But being afraid and clinging to control are potent forces, keeping patterns going long past their usefulness.

In the case of the near-disaster with my cat, it was with great ease, in the aftermath, that I saw I'd been overdoing it with economizing. Since then, my electric bill may be a tad higher than before. But the *cost* of saving money is dear beyond measure, when it involves risk to one I love.

We are only ever going along for the ride. Life introduces a new curriculum, whenever one is called for. So long as we're attentive students in the classroom of the everyday, learning will never cease. There are teachers everywhere, always.

—⟋〰⟍—

When contemplating letting go of a thing I've been doing, perhaps something that's long been a part of my life, I reflect on the anticipated cost of doing so versus the perceived benefit. Maybe it's something dear to me that I didn't always realize carried a cost.

Singing in choirs had brought so much joy when I was young. Yet as an adult, absorbed in mothering and earning a living, I'd had precious little of the experience of singing with others. For some years in middle age, I'd wished I could join a wonderful local choir. But its rehearsal time conflicted with one of the creative writing workshops I facilitated. At long last I auditioned for the choir. What a happy day it was. Making the necessary sacrifice in my finances, I said goodbye to the Wednesday night writing group. Soon enough I was bringing music to life with a roomful of enthusiastic singers and a conductor to die for.

Being in the choir entailed driving to evening rehearsals. After several years of joyous participation, I noticed my sleep schedule gently changing, such that I now found myself waking around 3 am. Driving to rehearsals got me home close to 10 pm. It began to feel perilous: I could kill someone (like me) on the sleepy trip home. Despite multiple attempts to find a ride to and fro, there appeared to be no reasonable way to do that. And so I found myself telling the beloved conductor that I needed to withdraw from the group. While it was certainly a loss, there was no confusion whatever that the decision was wise.

Of course I was sad to have to say goodbye to an experience long hungered for. At the same time, I was surprised to notice something like relief in the aftermath. For in the learning of music new to me, I'd necessarily needed to engage my mind. Since I dearly loved singing virtually everything in our repertoire, I hadn't paid a lot of attention to the mental work it entailed. The bodied experience of joy had "muted" the sensation of effort. Still, I now saw there surely had been a cost. Had the delight justified the subtle exertion? Absolutely. Just the same, when I recognized the scale of the cost to continuing (someone could die), I had no trouble letting the choir go. Nor did I entertain prospects of altering my new sleep routine, which I had not chosen.

A kindred development occurred several years later, shocking to me and to many others. I'd been happily leading writing workshops for nearly 30 years. These creative gatherings constituted the most deeply satisfying paid work of my life. Most participants stayed with the groups for years. Imagine their surprise, then – and my own! – when out of the blue, I saw it was time to stop. I hadn't seen the change coming. I'd supposed this work would continue for as long as aging enabled me. Still, I knew not to turn away from the deep truth of what I had now seen, unaccountable as it was.

As it happened, that startling development occurred at a fortuitous moment. By then I'd been offering support to spiritual seekers for many years. The growing number of requests had brought about a situation (for I had two "jobs" filling my days) in which there was typically an interval of a few months between a request for a session and an opening. Letting go the workshops meant space would open up to accommodate seekers in a more timely way.

The writing groups had been an inadvertent blessing to some of those very seekers. In the months following my awakening, a good deal of the "processing" *(what-on-earth-has-happened?)* took place there. All my life, putting pen to paper has been the way I've explored new life developments. Although as facilitator I always offered a prompt to the assembled writers, I found myself unable to focus on anything but the mysterious thing going on inside me. After each writing period, each person would read aloud what had shown up on the page. The listeners would then offer reflections. However autobiographical the writing might appear to be, the material was to be treated as fiction, creating a boundary that established a safe environment for creative freedom. The guideline was always adhered to.

When I read my own words aloud during those life-altering months, sometimes I'd look up from my notebook to see stunned expressions on everyone's faces. The room was utterly still. Nor did anybody seem to know what to offer in the way of writerly feedback. I could see it in their eyes: *Something has happened to Jan.* Even so, the long-trusted rule obtained. The boundaries were honored.

Then one day a long-term writing companion, who was also a devoted meditator, approached me outside the workshop setting and asked whether she could gently step over that boundary. I said yes. We spoke of what was happening inside me.

One thing led to another after that. As word spread among the local community of seekers, there were growing requests for me to assemble the material into a volume. Until then, I'd had no plan for a book. Let alone did I ever intend to become a spiritual teacher. The next thing I knew, several publishers wanted the manuscript. The one I chose indicated that I would need a website so people would be able to contact me. While I protested that I didn't want a website, she insisted there would be a need for one. Reluctantly, I caved in.

It appears she was right.

—ɯ—

## Processing

Life happens fast. The irony is noteworthy: while a given moment is utterly still (when you're really there), the succession of lived nows, when the mind revisits a stretch of time, appears to have occurred with lightning speed. Just ask anybody who's old – most poignantly, one on their death bed. The impression of speed grows with the accumulation of years: for a single one is but an ever-shrinking proportion of the entirety.

Where did it all go?

I sit facing my brother. I drink in his lovely old face, the dear voice, everything about him its same familiar self, however the years pile on. Some things don't change. We've been close all our lives, sharing deeply about music, about what it is to live with integrity, about the nature of the vastness beyond this existence. My brother and I have said things to one another we've shared with not another soul. I listen to his halting portrayal of how life feels now. When he reaches for his cup of coffee, I watch his hand tremble. At moments it's apparent he's lost his train of thought.

All my life my brother has been beloved, he who at the start (because born some years prior) was a role model to the earnest youthful me. He played a major part in shaping me into the person I would become, opening doors through which I joyfully stepped. He led me to the luscious world of classical music – not via anything ever said, but by example. Handel and Brahms poured from behind the shut bedroom door of my big brother. It was clear he reveled in that world. How could I too not enter it? Our age difference, then, was significant. Six years counts for a lot when you're kids.

Though we haven't lived near one another for decades, he and I have always managed to visit, to spend quiet time together, sharing deeply about things of kindred concern. Never have we resorted to the trivial, nor was there ever sibling tension.

Both of us, now, are old. Over the era of our grown-up encounters, the age difference was irrelevant, not apparent. But in these recent days together, my brother seems again to be my elder. Now I am looking out for he who once tended me: for my dear brother is diminished, physically and mentally. He has changed a good deal since we last sat together, not many months ago. My mind registers the change, and I happily accommodate his needs of the moment, adapting with ease as the moment asks. Just the same, I'm aware, as we sit companionably, that once he's returned home, there will be a good deal for me to take account of.

Now, blessed now, what's primary is that he is here. We are together, in this cherished moment.

—⁓—

One thing I've discovered in recent years is that life itself, moment to moment, occurs much more quickly than the processing of it. When I'm having an encounter with my son or daughter over the course of hours or days, much gets shared and felt. I listen deeply. My eyes drink in the face of my beloved grown-up child. I've learned that the taking-it-in wants every drop of attention, especially if they're speaking of something significant, whose content embodies rich feeling or insight. Were I to try to process such an encounter while it's under way, I simply would not be there for the next said thing. Inside my attuned body, the present-moment experience engages my heart, a little of my mind. We are in the now together.

Life itself occurs with breathtaking speed. Each moment is fleeting *(now, now, now)*, asking a purity of attunement. If I'm listening to a loved one describe how much something matters, or how painful it is, and my attention diverts to the thing's perceived ramifications, I'll miss something. The registering of anything significant takes longer than whatever has precipitated it. This is particularly true in the case of a big change. In no way would it be desirable to experience and simultaneously to take account of. Each merits full attention – the lived reality, and the way it takes up residence in the receiving heart and mind.

When I initially understood this many years ago, it was a revelation. I found that if I tried to register concurrently a thing being heard or observed, I'd inevitably miss the next moment. Because I didn't want to miss any of the actual encounter, I began to postpone the secondary experience until its aftermath.

It took a while for me to cease attempting to process, mid-life-experience, all I was feeling and seeing. I learned the hard way: for I became aware that if I "stepped back" from the swiftly unfolding moment to grant the heart its longed-for space, *I would miss what was happening now.* I wouldn't hear what was being said. I'd miss a good deal of the precious time with a loved one. The cost of attempting to do both at once is dear. At bottom, it is not kind to myself (or to my beloved child, or my brother) to do anything but purely attend.

What I came to understand was that I was actually attempting to multitask: to experience and concurrently to process. Once I realized that, and saw the cost of not being fully present with what was happening in the now, I tenderly granted myself permission to wait until the solitude and the silence of *after,* to allow all the necessary space asked by the savoring heart. This is one of the reasons I need a good deal of spaciousness in my daily life, why a good deal of unstructured time is essential.

This sort of processing wants the generosity of a stretch of time, occurring not in the background but very much in the fore of conscious awareness. A time of reckoning, as occurred after the encounter with my brother, asks plenty of space to enable something new and altering to register. It's to take account of a change. It is to feel, to look away from nothing.

It is also to notice any impulse to protect oneself. The habitual tendency is to avert the eyes from a surprising or unwelcome new reality. There may be the seeking of refuge in how it was before, until now. A person may be desperate to avoid the discomfort of a fully-reckoning heart. (Once, that person would have been me.) To allow in the newness is to incorporate it into oneself, enabling a moving ahead. As life carries on, the nowadays "image" of a loved one, a relationship, is fully in the picture. To do this is to play with a full deck.

Surprisingly, it is only a blessing when the lifelong inclination to look away from a painful truth – a thing unwanted, unanticipated – has ceased functioning. The strongest impulse, ever after, is to look the truth squarely in the face. All our lives we have ached for stability and comfort. For as T.S. Eliot observes:

> *human kind*
> *Cannot bear very much reality.*

While we've done it to spare ourselves acute discomfort, the persistent habit of looking away from evidence to the contrary has in fact only intensified the underlying strain of living. For on some level, we've long silently suspected we've been lying to ourselves. At long last, the actual truth – even when it's difficult – is a peaceful place to come to rest. This is one of the blessings of what it is to be awake. It's to be entirely aligned with reality, which includes ceaseless change.

Part of what it is to live is to feel how everything changes, moment to fleeting moment. In an encounter that deeply matters, to live is to really be here, while the experience is unfolding. During those precious days with my brother, had I been fully integrating his evident changes, I would have missed something. I was aware that plenty of space would be needed in the aftermath, to allow all I'd observed to register.

What if this time together were to turn out to be our last? One day it will be. Though seldom is such an encounter seen for what it is, while it's under way. Such things tend to be realized only in wistful (often regretful) retrospect. *If only,* we lament.

We owe it to ourselves to hold still for a thing that deeply matters, whether it shimmers with pain or joy, or with some of each. This is what it is to have a human life, to be endowed with a heart. Sometimes the tender heart simply needs to break. Tears long to be allowed to breach their tight doors.

I am done with lamenting. Let us all be done! There's nothing to do but fully be in the now. Let *after* take care of itself. Mortal life is fleeting. In the realm of embodied existence, time is indeed real – and brief.

—⟁—

## The Fun of Being a Person

All my life I have loved words, their meanings, how to spell them. This is a feature of my embodied self, shaped (as is the case for each of us) by genetic endowment and by the environment my birth landed me in. The compelling occupation, early on, was the tactile experience of curling my small fingers around a fat pencil and bringing letters into being. I studied earnestly to prepare for spelling bees. Early on, being a wordsmith, I became a devotee of Scrabble and crossword puzzles. Anyone observing would have foretold two inevitabilities: I would be a writer, and I would major in English.

Scrabble-playing, as it is for me since awakening, nicely illumines the difference between before and after. Historically, beginning in early childhood, I was not only skillful with all things relating to words – spelling, grammar, writing – but also ferociously identified with that strength. Hence the enduring memories I hold of all the youthful spelling bees I didn't quite win, and in each case who beat me (and with which word). I never forgot it was the red-headed girl who knew how *hygiene* was spelled. Somewhat later, I earnestly crafted poems, just as devotedly sending them to literary journals in the hope of their being accepted. On the infrequent and joyous occasion when an acceptance letter landed in the rusty mailbox out by the road, I shrieked to the sky. My children still remember their mother doing that when they were little. They could hear it from inside the house: it was the sound of Mom-being-happy. Getting into a good journal meant I was A Good Poet, and that mattered almost as much as the keen pleasure of writing a poem.

Imagine my surprise, then, when I later ceased being attached to praise or success. Sometimes a reader of one of my books will say positive things about its impact or about my writing ability. While I'm glad to know the book is helpful, nothing in me feels the long-familiar surge of self-worth. When something you're good at is admired or complimented by another, and that positive reinforcement has no impact whatever on how you feel – well, after a lifelong association between praise and a stroked ego, it is strange to be sure.

Waking up doesn't undo skills that are part of our "endowment," whether genetic or based on conditioning. What it does is free us of *attachment* to our gifts. They no longer define us. We don't identify with something we happen to be good at. A book is not an extension of me, puffing up my identity. I continue to enjoy writing, or I wouldn't be writing this book. It's just that I no longer take pride in the outcome. An activity may still be fun (as Scrabble is, in my case).

As it happens, this very morning I came upon the word *zephyrs*. The Scrabble devotee in me registered that it would be a killer word to play: using all seven letters (yielding an extra 50 points), including the 10-point Z and two additional high-scoring letters. These kinds of words still get my attention, as they have since girlhood, but not because I'm any longer hellbent on getting the highest score. I don't care who wins now; I often don't even notice who's ahead, as a game is under way. Just the same, the lifelong delight in making a good word is intact. And (yes) I'm still good at it. It's fun!

Nowadays, my daughter often beats me at Scrabble. She has learned well from her mother, as I did from my own. Nothing could please me more.

She and I sit side by side on the cabin porch. A few days each summer, we come here to camp. This is one of our favorite places in the world. At present a heavy rain falls just a few feet from our faces, but we are dry beneath the wide eave. The gray curtain of water mutes our view of the lake, out there in the near distance. It's a chilly morning. We're bundled up in hooded sweatshirts, sipping hot drinks. It looks like a Scrabble day. The travel board is splayed open on the table between our wooden chairs.

Neither of us minds that it doesn't look like a day for swimming in the lake, or in the pool with the fun slide and the joyous screaming kids. We won't be out in the kayak this time, watching turtles bake themselves on warm stones, green feet stretched behind them. Or beavers breaking the surface, then going back under. We won't see the beauteous loons fishing not far from our inflatable boats, their beaks arcing down and up again. Nor do we lament there'll likely be no campfire this evening.

How is it that a rainy day of camping truly is okay? But it is. When we sit together like this, each of us is her most real self.

That's why we love it here. No matter the weather, whatever we may be doing.

Not many weeks later, she and I are on a train making a vast right angle across the country, first up and then, at Chicago, angling to the right, home to New England. We're on our way back from the Grand Canyon. This time we sit facing, the portable wooden Scrabble board opened out between us. The rocking under our bodies is delicious, familiar. By now the ceaseless motion feels normal, like home. Later, when our feet land back on terra firma, after so many days of rolling momentum, thousands of miles of it, the still ground beneath us will feel weird, almost alien.

The mournful song of the train whistle pierces our hearts, the landscape rushing along above our word game. The horizontal glass is an ever-changing movie screen. Each time we glance up, the scenery has changed. We take turns forming words from the pale wooden tiles, tally up the points. She's just now played, and I'm shuffling the miniature tiles on my own tiny tray.

Now the opening bars of one of my favorite-ever songs begin animating the air around our heads. Arlo Guthrie is singing *City of New Orleans*. I look up to see my daughter holding her phone, smiling. She has uploaded the song, knowing how her mother loves that music about riding on a train.

Through my tears I look into those tender green eyes. Her generosity knows no bounds. This is the way it is with us.

These recent months I've watched my daughter move with gathering momentum into her life. What a pleasure it is to witness her taking on grueling academic challenges, in pursuit of her heart's desire: to become a physician. Her devotion is palpable, her dedication admirable.

Meanwhile, as she is full steam ahead, my own "wheels" are slowing. Both of us are keenly aware of the brevity of the era of our leisurely togetherness. For now, I am energetic and reasonably fit. For the time being, though she is significantly busier than she's ever been, she still lives fairly close by. Though that will surely change before long. And so, in the winding-down times of our overlapping availability, we're making hay, seizing whatever opportunity presents itself.

Whatever the circumstances, it's all brief, for every one of us. Arlo helps us remember:

*This train's got the disappearing railroad blues.*

While we're still on it, there's nothing for a mother to do but sing.

Which I do.

# Epilogue

Where did it all go? We ask this not just when death is staring us down, but near the end of an eagerly-anticipated vacation, a visit with a cherished friend or family member. Is it over already?

Were we paying attention as each moment unfolded? Were we really there? Never has anyone asked this with a more piercing urgency than a character in Thornton Wilder's *Our Town:*

> *Do any human beings ever realize life while*
> *they live it – every, every minute?*

The wistful speaker of those words is dead. However belatedly, she finally gets it.

How can we avert our eyes? Yet we do, all our lives. When will we stop being surprised by the fleetingness and truly, at long and delicious last, live?

The desire to spiritually awaken is often launched by the wish to stop hurting. The mind insists a journey is needed to get there. Sometimes there may be a visceral knowing that there's something innate to us that's already free.

That is to be trusted.

Many a seeker spends years on the "journey," eyes cast above the head of one precious now after another, fixated on the fabled land of freedom. Chances are, they'll end up where so many do on their death bed. *Where did it go?*

This is what it comes down to, dear heart: to know the present for the jewel it is, however imperfect or unremarkable it may appear.

Don't make awakening into something grand, beyond the physical, the oh-so-human. Stop the infernal seeking after an idea in your head. If you imagine waking up ends the experience of the breaking heart, you're deluding yourself.

When they say "You're already there, you just don't know it," maybe they know what they're talking about. What you ache for is right here. Feel yourself being in this moment of life, whatever it holds. Be still. Breathe. Tune in to your beating heart. If it wants to break, let it.

Maybe when Ram Dass said "Be here now," he knew what he was talking about. (Notice he did not say "Be here now *if all's well*.")

—⁂—

It's Christmas time. My house is filled with Handel's *Messiah*, dearly familiar from my long life of choral singing. Now comes the rapturous soprano solo, for me the heart of the piece. Though my alto voice strains for the high notes, I cannot help but sing.

*Come unto Him, all ye that labor, that are heavy laden,*
*and He will give you rest.*

How to produce sound with tears streaming down my face? It's always this way, since the long-ago moment I finally understood the man who's said to have been the son of God.

The soprano's words are ascribed to Jesus Christ, but what they express comes as truly from my own heart. How I long for all who suffer to know the truth of what they are, to rest at last in radical love. This is what Jesus wanted us to know: that we are all what he was. No, I'm not a Christian. (Neither was he.)

It's about being so immersed in a piece of music that you *are* the music. About pausing to take in the glory of a sunrise, its color and motion unfolding before your dying eyes. Because you know this is the only chance you'll ever get for *this*. In the crucial matter of not-failing-to-live, these moments could be our teachers.

Why do they mostly not end up teaching us? Unlike a musical composition, which endures just a handful of minutes, and unlike a sunrise, gone in the blink of an enraptured eye, the river of life carries on and on, one day mostly undifferentiated from the next. It's so easy to take the present for granted, to miss it as it flies by. Something in us manages not to register the precious moment-to-moment of it all. We don't notice how a day, an hour, is constructed of thousands of nows. It's tragically easy to not see, to not-live and not-live. Then arrives the startling nearness of death. If we're conscious, we cannot fathom where it all went.

It ran down the drain, courtesy of the mind's plumbing, perpetually reaching past the present to one-fine-day. What could be more tragic? When ordinary life was a piece of music, a single sustained sunrise, struggling to get our attention every moment of our brief existence. There is no finer doorway to the truth than relaxing into the arms of the now. That's all awakening ever was about.

Stop trying to fix yourself. Live.

## Leaving Bethlehem

Not that someone needed to die for our sins,
or that wandering men followed a star
across the chilled desert
to locate a newborn nestled in a trough,
surrounded by animals
stupefied
by what they saw in the baby's eyes.
This is not what I take from Christmas,
though it has its point.

But what the sheep and the cow saw,
what made the donkey
lower her eyes
and worry the hay floor with her hoof,
nervous and changed –
that's what goads me on,
what keeps my feet moving over the cold sand,
hunting this holy thing
that God left out

of nothing.

*1993*

*With thanks to my daughter Laura
for the glorious photograph of the Grand Canyon
and the one of me at Walden Pond*

*and*

*To my brother Jim
for his keen editorial eye*

# References

## *Epigraph*

Henry David Thoreau, *Walden* (Dodd, Mead & Company, 1946).

## *First Things First*

Eckhart Tolle, *The Power of Now* (New World Library, 1999).

*When Fear Falls Away: The Story of a Sudden Awakening* (Weiser Books, 2007).

*The Freedom of Being: At Ease with What Is* (Weiser Books, 2012).

*Opening the Door: Jan Frazier Teachings on Awakening* (eBookIt, 2012).

*The Great Sweetening: Life After Thought* (eBookIt, 2017 and 2016).

## *The Beginning: October 2019*

Herman Melville, *Moby-Dick; or The Whale* (Harper & Brothers, 1851).

## *Life Since: As of 2022*

Bill Whelan, "Caoineadh Cú Chulainn," *Riverdance,* Celtic Heartbeat, 1995.

T.S. Eliot, *Four Quartets,* in *T.S. Eliot: Collected Poems 1909-1962* (Harcourt, Brace & World, 1930).

Dante Alighieri, *The Inferno,* in *Divine Comedy* (Paradiso, 2021).

Robert Frost, "Stopping by Woods on a Snowy Evening," in *The Poetry of Robert Frost: The Collected Poems* (Holt, Rinehart and Winston, 1969).

Arlo Guthrie, "The City of New Orleans," *Hobo's Lullaby*, Warner Bros. Records Inc., 1972. (Composed by Steve Goodman © Kama Rippa Music Turnpike Tom)

## *Epilogue*

Thornton Wilder, *Our Town* (Harper Perennial, 2003).

Ram Dass, *Be Here Now* (Lama Foundation, 1971).